THE WILD DUCK

By Henrik Ibsen

Translated by Frances E. Archer

A Digireads.com Book
Digireads.com Publishing
16212 Riggs Rd
Stilwell, KS, 66085

The Wild Duck
By Henrik Ibsen
Translated by Frances E. Archer
ISBN: 1-4209-3085-0

Please visit *www.digireads.com*

CHARACTERS

WERLE, *a merchant, manufacturer, etc.*
GREGERS WERLE, *his son.*
OLD EKDAL. HIALMAR EKDAL, *his son, a photographer.*
GINA EKDAL, *Hialmar's wife.*
HEDVIG, *their daughter, a girl of fourteen.*
MRS. SÖRBY, *WERLE's housekeeper.*
RELLING, *a doctor.*
MOLVIK, *student of theology.*
GRÅBERG, *WERLE's bookkeeper.*
PETTERSEN, *WERLE's servant.*
JENSEN, *a hired waiter.*
A FLABBY GENTLEMAN.
A THIN-HAIRED GENTLEMAN.
A SHORT-SIGHTED GENTLEMAN.
Six other gentlemen, guests at WERLE's dinner-party.
Several hired waiters.

The first act passes in Werle's house, the remaining acts at Hialmar Ekdal's.

Pronunciation of Names: Gregers Werle = Grayghers Verlë; Hialmar Ekdal = Yalmar Aykdal; Gina = Gheena; Gråberg = Groberg; Jensen = Yensen.

THE WILD DUCK

PLAY IN FIVE ACTS

ACT I.

At WERLE'S *house. A richly and comfortably furnished study; bookcases and upholstered furniture; a writing-table, with papers and documents, in the centre of the room; lighted lamps with green shades, giving a subdued light. At the back, open folding-doors with curtains drawn back. Within is seen a large and handsome room, brilliantly lighted with lamps and branching candle-sticks. In front, on the right (in the study), a small baize door leads into* WERLE'S *Office. On the left, in front, a fireplace with a glowing coal fire, and farther back a double door leading into the dining-room.*

WERLE'S *servant,* PETTERSEN, *in livery, and* JENSEN, *the hired waiter, in black, are putting the study in order. In the large room, two or three other hired waiters are moving about, arranging things and lighting more candles. From the dining-room, the hum of conversation and laughter of many voices are heard; a glass is tapped with a knife; silence follows, and a toast is proposed; shouts of "Bravo!" and then again a buzz of conversation.*

PETTERSEN. (*Lights a lamp on the chimney-place and places a shade over it.*). Hark to them, Jensen! now the old man's on his legs holding a long palaver about Mrs. Sörby.

JENSEN. (*Pushing forward an arm-chair.*). Is it true, what folks say, that they're—very good friends, eh?

PETTERSEN. Lord knows.

JENSEN. I've heard tell as he's been a lively customer in his day.

PETTERSEN. May be.

JENSEN. And he's giving this spread in honour of his son, they say.

PETTERSEN. Yes. His son came home yesterday.

JENSEN. This is the first time I ever heard as Mr. Werle had a son.

PETTERSEN. Oh yes, he has a son, right enough. But he's a fixture, as you might say, up at the Höidal works. He's never once come to town all the years I've been in service here.

A WAITER. (*In the doorway of the other room.*). Pettersen, here's an old fellow wanting—

PETTERSEN. (*Mutters.*) The devil—who's this now?

> OLD EKDAL *appears from the right, in the inner room. He is dressed in a threadbare overcoat with a high collar; he wears woollen mittens, and carries in his hand a stick and a fur cap. Under his arm, a brown paper parcel. Dirty red-brown wig and small grey moustache.*

PETTERSEN. (*Goes towards him.*) Good Lord—what do you want here?

EKDAL. (*In the doorway.*) Must get into the office, Pettersen.

PETTERSEN. The office was closed an hour ago, and—

EKDAL. So they told me at the front door. But Gråberg's in there still. Let me slip in this way, Pettersen; there's a good fellow. (*Points towards the baize door.*) It's not the first time I've come this way.

PETTERSEN. Well, you may pass. (*Opens the door.*) But mind you go out again the proper way, for we've got company.

EKDAL. I know, I know—h'm! Thanks, Pettersen, good old friend! Thanks! (*Mutters softly.*) Ass!

He goes into the Office; PETTERSEN *shuts the door after him.*

JENSEN. Is he one of the office people?

PETTERSEN. No he's only an outside hand that does odd jobs of copying. But he's been a tip-topper in his day, has old Ekdal.

JENSEN. You can see he's been through a lot.

PETTERSEN. Yes; he was an army officer, you know.

JENSEN. You don't say so?

PETTERSEN. No mistake about it. But then he went into the timber trade or something of the sort. They say he once played Mr. WERLE a very nasty trick. They were partners in the Höidal works at the time. Oh, I know old Ekdal well, I do. Many a nip of bitters and bottle of ale we two have drunk at Madam Eriksen's.

JENSEN. He don't look as if held much to stand treat with.

PETTERSEN. Why, bless you, Jensen, it's me that stands treat. I always think there's no harm in being a bit civil to folks that have seen better days.

JENSEN. Did he go bankrupt then?

PETTERSEN. Worse than that. He went to prison.

JENSEN. To prison!

PETTERSEN. Or perhaps it was the Penitentiary. (*Listens.*) Sh! They're leaving the table.

> *The dining-room door is thrown open from within, by a couple of waiters.* MRS. SÖRBY *comes out conversing with two gentlemen. Gradually the whole company follows, amongst them* WERLE. *Last come* HIALMAR EKDAL *and* GREGERS WERLE.

MRS. SÖRBY. (*In passing, to the servant.*) Tell them to serve the coffee in the music-room, Pettersen.

PETTERSEN. Very well, Madam.

> *She goes with the two Gentlemen into the inner room, and thence out to the right.* PETTERSEN *and* JENSEN *go out the same way.*

A FLABBY GENTLEMAN. (*To a* THIN-HAIRED GENTLEMAN.) Whew! What a dinner!—It was no joke to do it justice!

THE THIN-HAIRED GENTLEMAN. Oh, with a little good-will one can get through a lot in three hours.

THE FLABBY GENTLEMAN. Yes, but afterwards, afterwards, my dear Chamberlain!

A THIRD GENTLEMAN. I hear the coffee and maraschino are to be served in the music-room.

THE FLABBY GENTLEMAN. Bravo! Then perhaps Mrs. Sörby will play us something.

THE THIN-HAIRED GENTLEMAN. (*In a low voice.*) I hope Mrs. Sörby mayn't play us a tune we don't like, one of these days!

THE FLABBY GENTLEMAN. Oh no, not she! Bertha will never turn against her old friends.

> *They laugh and pass into the inner room.*

WERLE. (*In a low voice, dejectedly.*) I don't think anybody noticed it, Gregers.

GREGERS. (*Looks at him.*) Noticed what?

WERLE. Did you not notice it either?

GREGERS. What do you mean?

WERLE. We were thirteen at table.

GREGERS. Indeed? Were there thirteen of us?

WERLE. (*Glances towards* HIALMAR EKDAL.) Our usual party is twelve. (*To the others*.) This way, gentlemen!

    WERLE *and the others, all except* HIALMAR *and* GREGERS, *go out by the back, to the right.*

HIALMAR. (*Who has overheard the conversation.*) You ought not to have invited me, Gregers.

GREGERS. What! Not ask my best and only friend to a party supposed to be in my honour—?

HIALMAR. But I don't think your father likes it. You see I am quite outside his circle.

GREGERS. So I hear. But I wanted to see you and have a talk with you, and I certainly shan't be staying long.—Ah, we two old schoolfellows have drifted far apart from each other. It must be sixteen or seventeen years since we met.

HIALMAR. Is it so long?

GREGERS. It is indeed. Well, how goes it with you? You look well. You have put on flesh, and grown almost stout.

HIALMAR. Well, "stout" is scarcely the word; but I daresay I look a little more of a man than I used to.

GREGERS. Yes, you do; your outer man is in first-rate condition.

HIALMAR. (*In a tone of gloom.*) Ah, but the inner man! That is a very different matter, I can tell you! Of course you know of the terrible catastrophe that has befallen me and mine since last we met.

GREGERS. (*More softly.*) How are things going with your father now?

HIALMAR. Don't let us talk of it, old fellow. Of course my poor unhappy father lives with me. He hasn't another soul in the world to care for him. But you can understand that this is a miserable subject for me.—Tell me, rather, how you have been getting on up at the works.

GREGERS. I have had a delightfully lonely time of it—plenty of leisure to think and think about things. Come over here; we may as well make ourselves comfortable.

He seats himself in an arm-chair by the fire and draws HIALMAR *down into another alongside of it.*

HIALMAR. (S*entimentally.*) After all, Gregers, I thank you for inviting me to your father's table; for I take it as a sign that you have got over your feeling against me.

GREGERS. (*Surprised.*) How could you imagine I had any feeling against you?

HIALMAR. You had at first, you know.

GREGERS. How at first?

HIALMAR. After the great misfortune. It was natural enough that you should. Your father was within an ace of being drawn into that—well, that terrible business.

GREGERS. Why should that give me any feeling against you? Who can have put that into your head?

HIALMAR. I know it did, Gregers; your father told me so himself.

GREGERS. (*Starts.*) My father! Oh indeed. H'm.—Was that why you never let me hear from you?—not a single word.

HIALMAR. Yes.

GREGERS. Not even when you made up your mind to become a photographer?

HIALMAR. Your father said I had better not write to you at all, about anything.

GREGERS. (*Looking straight before him.*) Well well, perhaps he was right.—But tell me now, Hialmar: are you pretty well satisfied with your present position?

HIALMAR. (*With a little sigh.*) Oh yes, I am; I have really no cause to complain. At first, as you may guess, I felt it a little strange. It was such a totally new state of things for me. But of course my whole circumstances were totally changed. Father's utter, irretrievable ruin,—the shame and disgrace of it, Gregers.—

GREGERS. (*Affected.*) Yes, yes; I understand.

HIALMAR. I couldn't think of remaining at college; there wasn't a shilling to spare; on the contrary, there were debts—mainly to your father I believe—

GREGERS. H'm—

HIALMAR. In short, I thought it best to break, once for all, with my old surroundings and associations. It was your father that specially urged me to it; and since he interested himself so much in me—

GREGERS. My father did?

HIALMAR. Yes, you surely knew that, didn't you? Where do you suppose I found the money to learn photography, and to furnish a studio and make a start? All that costs a pretty penny, I can tell you.

GREGERS. And my father provided the money?

HIALMAR. Yes, my dear fellow, didn't you know? I understood him to say he had written to you about it.

GREGERS. Not a word about his part in the business. He must have forgotten it. Our correspondence has always been purely a business one. So it was my father that—!

HIALMAR. Yes, certainly. He didn't wish it to be generally known; but he it was. And of course it was he, too, that put me in a position to marry. Don't you—don't you know about that either?

GREGERS. No, I haven't heard a word of it. (*Shakes him by the arm.*) But, my dear Hialmar, I can't tell you what pleasure all this gives me—pleasure, and self-reproach. I have perhaps done my father injustice after all—in some things. This proves that he has a heart. It shows a sort of compunction—

HIALMAR. Compunction—?

GREGERS. Yes, yes—whatever you like to call it. Oh, I can't tell you how glad I am to hear this of father.—So you are a married man, Hialmar! That is further than I shall ever get. Well, I hope you are happy in your married life?

HIALMAR. Yes, thoroughly happy. She is as good and capable a wife as any man could wish for. And she is by no means without culture.

GREGERS. (*Rather surprised.*) No, of course not.

HIALMAR. You see, life is itself an education. Her daily intercourse with me—And then we know one or two rather remarkable men, who come a good deal about us. I assure you, you would hardly know Gina again.

GREGERS. GINA?

HIALMAR. Yes; had you forgotten that her name was Gina?

GREGERS. Whose name? I haven't the slightest idea—

HIALMAR. Don't you remember that she used to be in service here?

GREGERS. (*Looks at him.*) Is it Gina Hansen—?

HIALMAR. Yes, of course it is Gina Hansen.

GREGERS.——who kept house for us during the last year of my mother's illness?

HIALMAR. Yes, exactly. But, my dear friend, I'm quite sure your father told you that I was married.

GREGERS. (*Who has risen.*) Oh yes, he mentioned it; but not that—(*Walking about the room.*) Stay—perhaps he did—now that I think of it. My father always writes such short letters. (*Half seats himself on the arm of the chair.*) Now, tell me, Hialmar— this is interesting—how did you come to know Gina—your wife?

HIALMAR. The simplest thing in the world. You know Gina did not stay here long, everything was so much upset at that time, owing to your mother's illness and so forth, that Gina was not equal to it all; so she gave notice and left. That was the year before your mother died—or it may have been the same year.

GREGERS. It was the same year. I was up at the works then. But afterwards—?

HIALMAR. Well, Gina lived at home with her mother, Madam Hansen, an excellent hard-working woman, who kept a little eating-house. She had a room to let too; a very nice comfortable room.

GREGERS. And I suppose you were lucky enough to secure it?

HIALMAR. Yes; in fact, it was your father that recommended it to me. So it was there, you see, that I really came to know Gina.

GREGERS. And then you got engaged?

HIALMAR. Yes. It doesn't take young people long to fall in love——; h'm——

GREGERS. (*Rises and moves about a little.*) Tell me: was it after your engagement—was it then that my father—I mean was it then that you began to take up photography?

HIALMAR. Yes, precisely. I wanted to make a start, and to set up house as soon as possible; and your father and I agreed that this photography business was the readiest way. Gina thought so too. Oh, and there was another thing in its favour, by-the-bye: it happened, luckily, that Gina had learnt to retouch.

GREGERS. That chimed in marvellously.

HIALMAR. (*Pleased, rises.*) Yes, didn't it? Don't you think it was a marvellous piece of luck?

GREGERS. Oh, unquestionably. My father seems to have been almost a kind of providence for you.

HIALMAR. (*With emotion.*) He did not forsake his old friend's son in the hour of his need. For he has a heart. you see.

MRS. SÖRBY. (*Enters, arm-in-arm with* WERLE.) Nonsense, my dear Mr. Werle; you mustn't stop there any longer staring at all the lights. It's very bad for you.

WERLE. (*Lets go her arm and passes his hand over his eyes.*) I daresay you are right.

PETTERSEN *and* JENSEN *carry round refreshment trays.*

MRS. SÖRBY. (*To the Guests in the other room.*) This way, if you please, gentlemen. Whoever wants a glass of punch must be so good as to come in here.

THE FLABBY GENTLEMAN. (*Comes up to* MRS. SÖRBY.*)* Surely, it isn't possible that you have suspended our cherished right to smoke?

MRS. SÖRBY. Yes. No smoking here, in Mr. Werle's sanctum, Chamberlain.

THE THIN-HAIRED GENTLEMAN. When did you enact these stringent amendments on the cigar law, Mrs. Sörby?

MRS. SÖRBY. After the last dinner, Chamberlain, when certain persons permitted themselves to overstep the mark.

THE THIN-HAIRED GENTLEMAN. And may one never overstep the mark a little bit, Madame Bertha? Not the least little bit?

MRS. SÖRBY. Not in any respect whatsoever, Mr. Balle.

Most of the Guests have assembled in the study; servants hand round glasses of Punch.

WERLE. (*To* HIALMAR, *who is standing beside a table.*) What are you studying so intently, Ekdal?

HIALMAR. Only an album, Mr. Werle.

THE THIN-HAIRED GENTLEMAN. (*Who is wandering about.*) Ah, photographs! They are quite in your line of course.

THE FLABBY GENTLEMAN. (*In an arm-chair.*) Haven't you brought any of your own with you?

HIALMAR. No, I haven't.

THE FLABBY GENTLEMAN. You ought to have; it's very good for the digestion to sit and look at pictures.

THE THIN-HAIRED GENTLEMAN. And it contributes to the entertainment, you know.

THE SHORT-SIGHTED GENTLEMAN. And all contributions are thankfully received.

MRS. SÖRBY. The Chamberlains think that when one is invited out to dinner, one ought to exert oneself a little in return, Mr. Ekdal.

THE FLABBY GENTLEMAN. Where one dines so well, that duty becomes a pleasure.

THE THIN-HAIRED GENTLEMAN. And when it's a case of the struggle for existence, you know—

MRS. SÖRBY. I quite agree with you!

They continue the conversation, with laughter and joking.

GREGERS. (*Softly.*) You must join in, Hialmar.

HIALMAR. (*Writhing.*) What am I to talk about?

THE FLABBY GENTLEMAN. Don't you think, Mr. Werle, that Tokay may be considered one of the more wholesome sorts of wine?

WERLE. (*By the fire.*) I can answer for the Tokay you had to-day, at any rate; it's one of the very finest seasons. Of course you would notice that.

THE FLABBY GENTLEMAN. Yes, it had a remarkably delicate flavour.

HIALMAR. (*Shyly.*) Is there any difference between the seasons?

THE FLABBY GENTLEMAN. (*Laughs.*) Come! That's good!

WERLE. (*Smiles.*) It really doesn't pay to set fine wine before you.

THE THIN-HAIRED GENTLEMAN. Tokay is like photographs, Mr. Ekdal: they both need sunshine. Am I not right?

HIALMAR. Yes, light is important no doubt.

MRS. SÖRBY. And it's exactly the same with Chamberlains—they, too, depend very much on sunshine, [1] as the saying is.

[1] The "sunshine" of Court favour

THE THIN-HAIRED GENTLEMAN. Oh fie! That's a very threadbare sarcasm!

THE SHORT-SIGHTED GENTLEMAN. Mrs. Sörby is coming out—

THE FLABBY GENTLEMAN.——and at our expense, too. (*Holds up his finger reprovingly.*) Oh, Madame Bertha, Madame Bertha!

MRS. SÖRBY. Yes, and there's not the least doubt that the seasons differ greatly. The old vintages are the finest.

THE SHORT-SIGHTED GENTLEMAN. Do you reckon me among the old vintages?

MRS. SÖRBY. Oh, far from it.

THE THIN-HAIRED GENTLEMAN. There now! But me, dear Mrs. Sörby—?

THE FLABBY GENTLEMAN. Yes, and me? What vintage should you say that we belong to?

MRS. SÖRBY. Why, to the sweet vintages, gentlemen.

She sips a glass of punch. The gentlemen laugh and flirt with her.

WERLE. Mrs. Sörby can always find a loop-hole—when she wants to. Fill your glasses, gentlemen! Pettersen, will you see to it—! GREGERS, suppose we have a glass together. (GREGERS *does not move.*) Won't you join us, Ekdal? I found no opportunity of drinking with you at table.

GRÅBERG, *the Bookkeeper, looks in at the baize door.*

GRÅBERG. Excuse me, sir, but I can't get out.

WERLE. Have you been locked in again?

GRÅBERG. Yes, and Flakstad has carried off the keys.

WERLE. Well, you can pass out this way.

GRÅBERG. But there's some one else—

WERLE. All right; come through, both of you. Don't be afraid.

GRÅBERG *and* OLD EKDAL *come out of the office.*

WERLE. (*Involuntarily.*) Ugh!

The laughter and talk among the Guests cease. HIALMAR starts at the sight of his father, puts down his glass, and turns towards the fireplace.

EKDAL. (*Does not look up, but makes little bows to both sides as he passes, murmuring.*) Beg pardon, come the wrong way. Door locked—door locked. Beg pardon.

He and GRÅBERG *go out by the back, to the right.*

WERLE. (*Between his teeth.*) That idiot GRÅBERG.

GREGERS. (*Open-mouthed and staring, to* HIALMAR.) Why surely that wasn't—!

THE FLABBY GENTLEMAN. What's the matter? Who was it?

GREGERS. Oh, nobody, only the bookkeeper and some one with him.

THE SHORT-SIGHTED GENTLEMAN. (*To* HIALMAR.) Did you know that man?

HIALMAR. I don't know—I didn't notice—

THE FLABBY GENTLEMAN. What the deuce has come over every one?

He joins another group who are talking softly.

MRS. SÖRBY. (*Whispers to the Servant.*) Give him something to take with him;—something good, mind.

PETTERSEN. (*Nods.*) I'll see to it. (*Goes out.*)

GREGERS. (*Softly and with emotion, to* HIALMAR.) So that was really he!

HIALMAR. Yes.

GREGERS. And you could stand there and deny that you knew him!

HIALMAR. (*Whispers vehemently.*) But how could I—!

GREGERS.—acknowledge your own father?

HIALMAR. (*With pain.*) Oh, if you were in my place—

The conversation amongst the Guests, which has been carried on in a low tone, now swells into constrained joviality.

THE THIN-HAIRED GENTLEMAN. (*Approaching* HIALMAR *and* GREGERS *in a friendly manner.*) Aha! Reviving old college memories, eh? Don't you smoke, Mr. Ekdal? May I give you a light? Oh, by-the-bye, we mustn't—

HIALMAR. No, thank you, I won't—

THE FLABBY GENTLEMAN. Haven't you a nice little poem you could recite to us, Mr. Ekdal? You used to recite so charmingly.

HIALMAR. I am sorry I can't remember anything.

THE FLABBY GENTLEMAN. Oh, that's a pity. Well, what shall we do, Balle?

Both Gentlemen move away and pass into the other room.

HIALMAR. (*Gloomily.*) Gregers—I am going! When a man has felt the crushing hand of Fate, you see—Say good-bye to your father for me.

GREGERS. Yes, yes. Are you going straight home?

HIALMAR. Yes. Why?

GREGERS. Oh, because I may perhaps look in on you later.

HIALMAR. No, you mustn't do that. You must not come to my home. Mine is a melancholy abode, Gregers; especially after a splendid banquet like this. We can always arrange to meet somewhere in the town.

MRS. SÖRBY. (*Who has quietly approached.*) Are you going, Ekdal?

HIALMAR. Yes.

MRS. SÖRBY. Remember me to Gina.

HIALMAR. Thanks.

MRS. SÖRBY. And say I am coming up to see her one of these days.

HIALMAR. Yes, thank you. (*To* GREGERS.) Stay here; I will slip out unobserved.

He saunters away, then into the other room, and so out to the right.

MRS. SÖRBY. (*Softly to the Servant, who has come back.*) Well, did you give the old man something?

PETTERSEN. Yes; I sent him off with a bottle of cognac.

MRS. SÖRBY. Oh, you might have thought of something better than that.

PETTERSEN. Oh no, Mrs. Sörby; cognac is what he likes best in the world.

THE FLABBY GENTLEMAN. (*In the doorway with a sheet of music in his hand.*) Shall we play a duet, Mrs. Sörby?

MRS. SÖRBY. Yes, suppose we do.

THE GUESTS. Bravo, bravo!

She goes with all the Guests through the back room, out to the right. GREGERS remains standing by the fire. WERLE is looking for Something on the writing-table, and appears to wish that GREGERS would go; as GREGERS does not move, WERLE goes towards the door.

GREGERS. Father, won't you stay a moment?

WERLE. (*Stops.*) What is it?

GREGERS. I must have a word with you.

WERLE. Can it not wait till we are alone?

GREGERS. No, it cannot; for perhaps we shall never be alone together.

WERLE. (*Drawing nearer.*) What do you mean by that?

During what follows, the pianoforte is faintly heard from the distant music-room.

GREGERS. How has that family been allowed to go so miserably to the wall?

WERLE. You mean the Ekdals, I suppose.

GREGERS. Yes, I mean the Ekdals. Lieutenant Ekdal was once so closely associated with you.

WERLE. Much too closely; I have felt that to my cost for many a year. It is thanks to him that I—yes I—have had a kind of slur cast upon my reputation.

GREGERS. (*Softly.*) Are you sure that he alone was to blame?

WERLE. Who else do you suppose—?

GREGERS. You and he acted together in that affair of the forests—

WERLE. But was it not Ekdal that drew the map of the tracts we had bought—that fraudulent map! It was he who felled all that timber illegally on Government ground. In fact, the whole management was in his hands. I was quite in the dark as to what Lieutenant Ekdal was doing.

GREGERS. Lieutenant Ekdal himself seems to have been very much in the dark as to what he was doing.

WERLE. That may be. But the fact remains that he was found guilty and I acquitted.

GREGERS. Yes, I know that nothing was proved against you.

WERLE. Acquittal is acquittal. Why do you rake up these old miseries that turned my hair grey before its time? Is that the sort of thing you have been brooding over up there, all these years? I can assure you, Gregers, here in the town the whole story has been forgotten long ago—so far as I am concerned.

GREGERS. But that unhappy Ekdal family—

WERLE. What would you have had me do for the people? When Ekdal came out of prison he was a broken-down being, past all help. There are people in the world who dive to the bottom the moment they get a couple of slugs in their body, and never come to the surface again. You may take my word for it, Gregers, I have done all I could without positively laying myself open to all sorts of suspicion and gossip—

GREGERS. Suspicion—? Oh, I see.

WERLE. I have given Ekdal copying to do for the office, and I pay him far, far more for it than his work is worth—

GREGERS. (*Without looking at him.*) H'm; that I don't doubt.

WERLE. You laugh? Do you think I am not telling you the truth? Well, I certainly can't refer you to my books, for I never enter payments of that sort.

GREGERS. (*Smiles coldly.*) No, there are certain payments it is best to keep no account of.

WERLE. (*Taken aback.*) What do you mean by t h a t?

GREGERS. (*Mustering up courage.*) Have you entered what it cost you to have Hialmar Ekdal taught photography?

WERLE. I? How "entered" it?

GREGERS. I have learnt that it was you who paid for his training. And I have learnt, too, that it was you who enabled him to set up house so comfortably.

WERLE. Well, and yet you talk as though I had done nothing for the Ekdals! I can assure you these people have cost me enough in all conscience.

GREGERS. Have you entered any of these expenses in your books?

WERLE. Why do you ask?

GREGERS. Oh, I have my reasons. Now tell me: when you interested yourself so warmly in your old friend's son—it was just before his marriage, was it not?

WERLE. Why, deuce take it—after all these years, how can I—?

GREGERS. You wrote me a letter about that time—a business letter, of course; and in a postscript you mentioned—quite briefly—that Hialmar Ekdal had married a Miss Hansen.

WERLE. Yes, that was quite right. That was her name.

GREGERS. But you did not mention that this Miss Hansen was Gina Hansen—our former housekeeper.

WERLE. (*With a forced laugh of derision.*) No; to tell the truth, it didn't occur to me that you were so particularly interested in our former housekeeper.

GREGERS. No more I was. But (*lowers his voice*) there were others in this house who were particularly interested in her.

WERLE. What do you mean by that? (*Flaring up.*) You are not alluding to me, I hope?

GREGERS. (*Softly but firmly.*) Yes, I am alluding to you.

WERLE. And you dare—! You presume to—! How can that ungrateful hound—that photographer fellow—how dare he go making such insinuations!

GREGERS. Hialmar has never breathed a word about this. I don't believe he has the faintest suspicion of such a thing.

WERLE. Then where have you got it from? Who can have put such notions in your head?

GREGERS. My poor unhappy mother told me; and that the very last time I saw her.

WERLE. Your mother! I might have known as much! You and she—you always held together. It was she who turned you against me, from the first.

GREGERS. No, it was all that she had to suffer and submit to, until she broke down and came to such a pitiful end.

WERLE. Oh, she had nothing to suffer or submit to; not more than most people, at all events. But there's no getting on with morbid, overstrained creatures—that I have learnt to my cost.—And you could go on nursing such a suspicion—burrowing into all sorts of old rumours and slanders against your own father! I must say, Gregers, I really think that at your age you might find something more useful to do.

GREGERS. Yes, it is high time.

WERLE. Then perhaps your mind would be easier than it seems to be now. What can be your object in remaining up at the works, year out and year in, drudging away like a common clerk, and not drawing a farthing more than the ordinary monthly wage? It is downright folly.

GREGERS. Ah, if I were only sure of that.

WERLE. I understand you well enough. You want to be independent; you won't be beholden to me for anything. Well, now there happens to be an opportunity for you to become independent, your own master in everything.

GREGERS. Indeed? In what way—?

WERLE. When I wrote you insisting on your coming to town at once—h'm—

GREGERS. Yes, what is it you really want of me? I have been waiting all day to know.

WERLE. I want to propose that you should enter the firm, as partner.

GREGERS. I! Join your firm? As partner?

WERLE. Yes. It would not involve our being constantly together. You could take over the business here in town, and I should move up to the works.

GREGERS. You would?

WERLE. The fact is, I am not so fit for work as I once was. I am obliged to spare my eyes, Gregers; they have begun to trouble me.

GREGERS. They have always been weak.

WERLE. Not as they are now. And, besides, circumstances might possibly make it desirable for me to live up there—for a time, at any rate.

GREGERS. That is certainly quite a new idea to me.

WERLE. Listen, Gregers: there are many things that stand between us; but we are father and son after all. We ought surely to be able to come to some sort of understanding with each other.

GREGERS. Outwardly, you mean, of course?

WERLE. Well, even that would be something. Think it over, Gregers. Don't you think it ought to be possible? Eh?

GREGERS. (*Looking at him coldly.*) There is something behind all this.

WERLE. How so?

GREGERS. You want to make use of me in some way.

WERLE. In such a close relationship as ours, the one can always be useful to the other.

GREGERS. Yes, so people say.

WERLE. I want very much to have you at home with me for a time. I am a lonely man, Gregers; I have always felt lonely, all my life through; but most of all now that I am getting up in years. I feel the need of some one about me—

GREGERS. You have Mrs. Sörby.

WERLE. Yes, I have her; and she has become, I may say, almost indispensable to me. She is lively and even-tempered; she brightens up the house; and that is a very great thing for me.

GREGERS. Well then, you have everything just as you wish it.

WERLE. Yes, but I am afraid it can't last. A woman so situated may easily find herself in a false position, in the eyes of the world. For that matter it does a man no good, either.

GREGERS. Oh, when a man gives such dinners as you give, he can risk a great deal.

WERLE. Yes, but how about the woman, Gregers? I fear she won't accept the situation much longer; and even if she did—even if, out of attachment to me, she were to take her chance of gossip and scandal and all that—? Do you think, Gregers—you with your strong sense of justice—

GREGERS. (*Interrupts him.*) Tell me in one word: are you thinking of marrying her?

WERLE. Suppose I were thinking of it? What then?

GREGERS. That's what I say: what then?

WERLE. Should you be inflexibly opposed to it!

GREGERS.—Not at all. Not by any means.

WERLE. I was not sure whether your devotion to your mother's memory—

GREGERS. I am not overstrained.

WERLE. Well, whatever you may or may not be, at all events you have lifted a great weight from my mind. I am extremely pleased that I can reckon on your concurrence in this matter.

GREGERS. (*Looking intently at him.*) Now I see the use you want to put me to.

WERLE. Use to put you to? What an expression!

GREGERS. Oh, don't let us be nice in our choice of words—not when we are alone together, at any rate. (*With a short laugh.*) Well well! So this is what made it absolutely essential that I should come to town in person. For the sake of Mrs. Sörby, we are to get up a pretence at family life in the house—a tableau of filial affection! That will be something new indeed.

WERLE. How dare you speak in that tone!

GREGERS. Was there ever any family life here? Never since I can remember. But now, forsooth, your plans demand something of the sort. No doubt it will have an excellent effect when it is reported that the son has hastened home, on the wings of filial piety, to the grey-haired father's wedding-feast. What will then remain of all the rumours as to the wrongs the poor dead mother had to submit to? Not a vestige. Her son annihilates them at one stroke.

WERLE. Gregers—I believe there is no one in the world you detest as you do me.

GREGERS. (*Softly.*) I have seen you at too close quarters.

WERLE. You have seen me with your mother's eyes. (*Lowers his voice a little.*) But you should remember that her eyes were—clouded now and then.

GREGERS. (*Quivering.*) I see what you are hinting at. But who was to blame for mother's unfortunate weakness? Why you, and all those—! The last of them was this woman that you palmed off upon Hialmar Ekdal, when you were—Ugh!

WERLE. (*Shrugs his shoulders.*) Word for word as if it were your mother speaking!

GREGERS. (*Without heeding.*) And there he is now, with his great, confiding, childlike mind, compassed about with all this treachery—living under the same roof with such a creature, and never dreaming that what he calls his home is built upon a lie! (*Comes a step nearer.*) When I look back upon your past, I seem to see a battle-field with shattered lives on every hand.

WERLE. I begin to think the chasm that divides us is too wide.

GREGERS. (*Bowing, with self-command.*) So I have observed; and therefore I take my hat and go.

WERLE. You are going! Out of the house?

GREGERS. Yes. For at last I see my mission in life.

WERLE. What mission?

GREGERS. You would only laugh if I told you.

WERLE. A lonely man doesn't laugh so easily, Gregers.

GREGERS. (*Pointing towards the background.*) Look, father,—the Chamberlains are playing blind-man's-buff with Mrs. Sörby.—Good-night and good-bye.

He goes out by the back to the right. Sounds of laughter and merriment from the Company, who are now visible in the outer room.

WERLE. (*Muttering contemptuously after* GREGERS.) Ha—! Poor wretch—and he says he is not overstrained!

ACT TWO.

HIALMAR EKDAL'S *studio, a good-sized room, evidently in the top storey of the building. On the right, a sloping roof of large panes of glass, half-covered by a blue curtain. In the right-hand corner, at the back, the entrance door; farther forward, on the same side, a door leading to the sitting-room. Two doors on the opposite side, and between them an iron stove. At the back, a wide double sliding-door. The studio is plainly but comfortably fitted up and furnished. Between the doors on the right, standing out a little from the wall, a sofa with a table and some chairs; on the table a lighted lamp with a shade; beside the stove an old arm-chair. Photographic instruments and apparatus of different kinds lying about the room. Against the back wall, to the left of the double door, stands a bookcase containing a few books, boxes, and bottles of chemicals, instruments, tools, and other objects. Photographs and small articles, such as camel's-hair pencils, paper, and so forth, lie on the table.*

GINA EKDAL *sits on a chair by the table, sewing.* HEDVIG *is sitting on the sofa, with her hands shading her eyes and her thumbs in her ears, reading a book.*

GINA. (*Glances once or twice at* HEDVIG, *as if with secret anxiety; then says.*): Hedvig!

HEDVIG (*Does not hear.*)

GINA. (*Repeats more loudly.*) Hedvig!

HEDVIG. (*Takes away her hands and looks up.*) Yes, mother?

GINA. Hedvig dear, you mustn't sit reading any longer now.

HEDVIG. Oh mother, mayn't I read a little more? Just a little bit?

GINA. No, no, you must put away your book now. Father doesn't like it; he never reads hisself in the evening.

HEDVIG. (*Shuts the book.*) No, father doesn't care much about reading.

GINA. (*Puts aside her sewing and takes up a lead pencil and a little account-book from the table.*) Can you remember how much we paid for the butter to-day?

HEDVIG. It was one crown sixty-five.

GINA. That's right. (*Puts it down.*) It's terrible what a lot of butter we get through in this house. Then there was the smoked sausage, and the cheese—let me see—(*Writes.*)—and the ham—(*Adds up.*) Yes, that makes just—

HEDVIG. And then the beer.

GINA. Yes, to be sure. (*Writes.*) How it do mount up! But we can't manage with no less.

HEDVIG. And then you and I didn't need anything hot for dinner, as father was out.

GINA. No; that was so much to the good. And then I took eight crowns fifty for the photographs.

HEDVIG. Really! So much as that?

GINA. Exactly eight crowns fifty.

Silence. GINA *takes up her sewing again,* HEDVIG *takes paper and pencil and begins to draw, shading her eyes with her left hand.*

HEDVIG. Isn't it jolly to think that father is at Mr. Werle's big dinner-party?

GINA. You know he's not really Mr. Werle's guest. It was the son invited him. (*After a pause.*) We have nothing to do with that Mr. Werle.

HEDVIG. I'm longing for father to come home. He promised to ask Mrs. Sörby for something nice for me.

GINA. Yes, there's plenty of good things going in that house, I can tell you.

HEDVIG. (*Goes on drawing.*) And I believe I'm a little hungry too.

OLD EKDAL, *with the paper parcel under his arm and another parcel in his coat pocket, comes in by the entrance door.*

GINA. How late you are to-day, grandfather!

EKDAL. They had locked the office door. Had to wait in Gråberg's room. And then they let me through—h'm.

HEDVIG. Did you get some more copying to do, grandfather?

EKDAL. This whole packet. Just look.

GINA. That's capital.

HEDVIG. And you have another parcel in your pocket.

EKDAL. Eh? Oh never mind, that's nothing. (*Puts his stick away in a corner.*) This work will keep me going a long time, Gina. (*Opens one of the sliding-doors in the back wall a little.*) Hush! (*Peeps into the room for a moment, then pushes the door carefully to again.*) Hee-hee! They're fast asleep, all the lot of them. And she's gone into the basket herself. Hee-hee!

HEDVIG. Are you sure she isn't cold in that basket, grandfather?

EKDAL. Not a bit of it! Cold? With all that straw? (*Goes towards the farther door on the left.*) There are matches in here, I suppose.

GINA. The matches is on the drawers.

EKDAL *goes into his room.*

HEDVIG. It's nice that grandfather has got all that copying.

GINA. Yes, poor old father; it means a bit of pocket-money for him.

HEDVIG. And he won't be able to sit the whole forenoon down at that horrid Madam Eriksen's.

GINA. No more he won't. (*Short silence.*)

HEDVIG. Do you suppose they are still at the dinner-table?

GINA. Goodness knows; as like as not.

HEDVIG. Think of all the delicious things father is having to eat! I'm certain he'll be in splendid spirits when he comes. Don't you think so, mother?

GINA. Yes; and if only we could tell him that we'd got the room let—

HEDVIG. But we don't need that this evening.

GINA. Oh, we'd be none the worst of it, I can tell you. It's no use to us as it is.

HEDVIG. I mean we don't need it this evening, for father will be in a good humour at any rate. It is best to keep the letting of the room for another time.

GINA. (*Looks across at her.*) You like having some good news to tell father when he comes home in the evening?

HEDVIG. Yes; for then things are pleasanter somehow.

GINA. (*Thinking to herself.*) Yes, yes, there's something in that.

OLD EKDAL *comes in again and is going out by the foremost door to the left.*

GINA. (*Half turning in her chair.*) Do you want something out of the kitchen, grandfather?

EKDAL. Yes, yes, I do. Don't you trouble. (*Goes out.*)

GINA. He's not poking away at the fire, is he? (*Waits a moment.*) Hedvig, go and see what he's about.

EKDAL *comes in again with a small jug of steaming hot water.*

HEDVIG. Have you been getting some hot water, grandfather?

EKDAL. Yes, hot water. Want it for something. Want to write, and the ink has got as thick as porridge—h'm.

GINA. But you'd best have your supper, first, grandfather. It's laid in there.

EKDAL. Can't be bothered with supper, Gina. Very busy, I tell you. No one's to come to my room. No one—h'm.

He goes into his room; GINA *and* HEDVIG *look at each other.*

GINA. (*Softly.*) Can you imagine where he's got money from?

HEDVIG. From Gråberg, perhaps.

GINA. Not a bit of it. Gråberg always sends the money to me.

HEDVIG. Then he must have got a bottle on credit somewhere.

GINA. Poor grandfather, who'd give him credit?

HIALMAR EKDAL, *in an overcoat and grey felt hat, comes in from the right.*

GINA. (*Throws down her sewing and rises.*) Why, Ekdal, Is that you already?

HEDVIG. (*At the same time jumping up.*) Fancy your coming so soon, father!

HIALMAR. (*Taking off his hat.*) Yes, most of the people were coming away.

HEDVIG. So early?

HIALMAR. Yes, it was a dinner-party, you know. (*Is taking off his overcoat.*)

GINA. Let me help you.

HEDVIG. Me too.

They draw off his coat; GINA *hangs it up on the back wall.*

HEDVIG. Were there many people there, father?

HIALMAR. Oh no, not many. We were about twelve or fourteen at table.

GINA. And you had some talk with them all?

HIALMAR. Oh yes, a little; but Gregers took me up most of the time.

GINA. Is Gregers as ugly as ever?

HIALMAR. Well, he's not very much to look at. Hasn't the old man come home?

HEDVIG. Yes, grandfather is in his room, writing.

HIALMAR. Did he say anything?

GINA. No, what should he say?

HIALMAR. Didn't he say anything about—? I heard something about his having been with Gråberg. I'll go in and see him for a moment.

GINA. No, no, better not.

HIALMAR. Why not? Did he say he didn't want me to go in?

GINA. I don't think he wants to see nobody this evening—

HEDVIG. (*Making signs.*) H'm—h'm!

GINA. (*Not noticing.*)—he has been in to fetch hot water—

HIALMAR. Aha! Then he's—

GINA. Yes, I suppose so.

HIALMAR. Oh God! my poor old white-haired father!—Well, well; there let him sit and get all the enjoyment he can.

OLD EKDAL, *in an indoor coat and with a lighted pipe, comes from his room.*

EKDAL. Got home? Thought it was you I heard talking.

HIALMAR. Yes, I have just come.

EKDAL. You didn't see me, did you?

HIALMAR. No, but they told me you had passed through—so I thought I would follow you.

EKDAL. H'm, good of you, Hialmar.—Who were they, all those fellows?

HIALMAR.—Oh, all sorts of people. There was Chamberlain Flor, and Chamberlain Balle, and Chamberlain Kaspersen, and Chamberlain—this, that, and the other—I don't know who all—

EKDAL. (*Nodding.*) Hear that, Gina! Chamberlains every one of them!

GINA. Yes, I hear as they're terrible genteel in that house nowadays.

HEDVIG. Did the Chamberlains sing, father? Or did they read aloud?

HIALMAR. No, they only talked nonsense. They wanted me to recite something for them; but I knew better than that.

EKDAL. You weren't to be persuaded, eh?

GINA. Oh, you might have done it.

HIALMAR. No; one mustn't be at everybody's beck and call. (*Walks about the room.*) That's not my way, at any rate.

EKDAL. No, no; Hialmar's not to be had for the asking, he isn't.

HIALMAR. I don't see why I should bother myself to entertain people on the rare occasions when I go into society. Let the others exert themselves. These fellows go from one great dinner-table to the next and gorge and guzzle day out and day in. It's for them to bestir themselves and do something in return for all the good feeding they get.

GINA. But you didn't say that?

HIALMAR. (*Humming.*) Ho-ho-ho—; faith, I gave them a bit of my mind.

EKDAL. Not the Chamberlains?

HIALMAR. Oh, why not? (*Lightly.*) After that, we had a little discussion about Tokay.

EKDAL. Tokay! There's a fine wine for you!

HIALMAR. (*Comes to a standstill.*) It may be a fine wine. But of course you know the vintages differ; it all depends on how much sunshine the grapes have had.

GINA. Why, you know everything, Ekdal.

EKDAL. And did they dispute that?

HIALMAR. They tried to; but they were requested to observe that it was just the same with Chamberlains—that with them, too, different batches were of different qualities.

GINA. What things you do think of!

EKDAL. Hee-hee! So they got that in their pipes too?

HIALMAR. Right in their teeth.

EKDAL. Do you hear that, Gina? He said it right in the very teeth of all the Chamberlains.

GINA. Fancy—! Right in their teeth!

HIALMAR. Yes, but I don't want it talked about. One doesn't speak of such things. The whole affair passed off quite amicably of course. They were nice, genial fellows; I didn't want to wound them—not I!

EKDAL. Right in their teeth, though—!

HEDVIG. (*Caressingly.*) How nice it is to see you in a dress-coat! It suits you so well, father.

HIALMAR. Yes, don't you think so? And this one really sits to perfection. It fits almost as if it had been made for me;—a little tight in the arm-holes perhaps;—help me, Hedvig (*takes off the coat.*) I think I'll put on my jacket. Where is my jacket, Gina?

GINA. Here it is. (*Brings the jacket and helps him.*)

HIALMAR. That's it! Don't forget to send the coat back to Molvik first thing to-morrow morning.

GINA. (*Laying it away.*) I'll be sure and see to it.

HIALMAR. (*Stretching himself.*) After all, there's a more homely feeling about this. A free-and-easy indoor costume suits my whole personality better. Don't you think so, Hedvig?

HEDVIG. Yes, father.

HIALMAR. When I loosen my necktie into a pair of flowing ends—like this?

HEDVIG. Yes, that goes so well with your moustache and the sweep of your curls.

HIALMAR. I should not call them curls exactly; I should rather say locks.

HEDVIG. Yes, they are too big for curls.

HIALMAR. Locks describes them better.

HEDVIG. (*After a pause, twitching his jacket.*) Father!

HIALMAR. Well, what is it?

HEDVIG. Oh, you know very well.

HIALMAR. No, really I don't—

HEDVIG. (*Half laughing, half whispering.*) Oh, yes, father; now don't tease me any longer!

HIALMAR. Why, what do you mean?

HEDVIG. (*Shaking him.*) Oh what nonsense; come, where are they, father? All the good things you promised me, you know?

HIALMAR. Oh—if I haven't forgotten all about them!

HEDVIG. Now you're only teasing me, father! Oh, it's too bad of you! Where have you put them?

HIALMAR. No, I positively forgot to get anything. But wait a little! I have something else for you, Hedvig. (*Goes and searches in the pockets of the coat.*)

HEDVIG. (*Skipping and clapping her hands.*) Oh mother, mother!

GINA. There, you see; if you only give him time—

HIALMAR. (*With a paper.*) Look, here it is.

HEDVIG. That? Why, that's only a paper.

HIALMAR. That is the bill of fare, my dear; the whole bill of fare. Here you see: "Menu"—that means bill of fare.

HEDVIG. Haven't you anything else?

HIALMAR. I forgot the other things, I tell you. But you may take my word for it, these dainties are very unsatisfying. Sit down at the table and read the bill of fare, and then I'll describe to you how the dishes taste. Here you are, Hedvig.

HEDVIG. (*Gulping down her tears.*) Thank you.

She seats herself, but does not read; GINA makes signs to her; HIALMAR notices it.

HIALMAR. (*Pacing up and down the room.*) It's monstrous what absurd things the father of a family is expected to think of; and if he forgets the smallest trifle, he is treated to sour faces at once. Well, well, one gets used to that too. (*Stops near the stove, by the old man's chair.*) Have you peeped in there this evening, father?

EKDAL. Yes, to be sure I have. She's gone into the basket.

HIALMAR. Ah, she has gone into the basket. Then she's beginning to get used to it.

EKDAL. Yes; just as I prophesied. But you know there are still a few little things—

HIALMAR. A few improvements, yes.

EKDAL. They've got to be made, you know.

HIALMAR. Yes, let us have a talk about the improvements, father. Come, let us sit on the sofa.

EKDAL. All right. H'm—think I'll just fill my pipe first. Must clean it out, too. H'm.

He goes into his room.

GINA. (*Smiling to* HIALMAR.) His pipe!

HIALMAR. Oh yes, yes, Gina; let him alone—the poor shipwrecked old man.—Yes, these improvements—we had better get them out of hand to-morrow.

GINA. You'll hardly have time to-morrow, Ekdal.

Hedvig. (*Interposing.*) Oh yes he will, mother!

GINA.——for remember them prints that has to be retouched; they've sent for them time after time.

HIALMAR. There now! those prints again! I shall get them finished all right! Have any new orders come in?

GINA. No, worse luck; to-morrow I have nothing but those two sittings, you know.

HIALMAR. Nothing else? Oh no, if people won't set about things with a will—

GINA. But what more can I do? Don't I advertise in the papers as much as we can afford?

HIALMAR. Yes, the papers, the papers; you see how much good they do. And I suppose no one has been to look at the room either?

GINA. No, not yet.

HIALMAR. That was only to be expected. If people won't keep their eyes open—. Nothing can be done without a real effort, Gina!

HEDVIG. (*Going towards him.*) Shall I fetch you the flute, father?

HIALMAR. No; no flute for me; I want no pleasures in this world. (*Pacing about.*) Yes, indeed I will work to-morrow; you shall see if I don't. You may be sure I shall work as long as my strength holds out.

GINA. But my dear good Ekdal, I didn't mean it in that way.

HEDVIG. Father, mayn't I bring in a bottle of beer?

HIALMAR. No, certainly not. I require nothing, nothing—(*Comes to a standstill.*) Beer? Was it beer you were talking about?

HEDVIG. (*Cheerfully.*) Yes, father; beautiful fresh beer.

HIALMAR. Well—since you insist upon it, you may bring in a bottle.

GINA. Yes, do; and we'll be nice and cosy.

HEDVIG *runs towards the kitchen door.*

HIALMAR. (*By the stove, stops her, looks at her, puts his arm round her neck and presses her to him.*) Hedvig, Hedvig!

HEDVIG. (*With tears of joy.*) My dear, kind father!

HIALMAR. No, don't call me that. Here have I been feasting at the rich man's table,—battening at the groaning board—! And I couldn't even—!

GINA. (*Sitting at the table.*) Oh, nonsense, nonsense, Ekdal.

HIALMAR. It's not nonsense! And yet you mustn't be too hard upon me. You know that I love you for all that.

HEDVIG. (*Throwing her arms round him.*) And we love you, oh, so dearly, father!

HIALMAR. And if I am unreasonable once in a while,—why then—you must remember that I am a man beset by a host of cares. There, there! (*Dries his eyes.*) No beer at such a moment as this. Give me the flute.

HEDVIG *runs to the bookcase and fetches it.*

HIALMAR. Thanks! That's right. With my flute in my hand and you two at my side—ah—!

HEDVIG *seats herself at the table near* GINA; HIALMAR *paces backwards and forwards, pipes up vigorously, and plays a Bohemian peasant-dance, but in a slow plaintive tempo, and with sentimental expression.*

HIALMAR. (*Breaking off the melody, holds out his left hand to* GINA, *and says with emotion.*): Our roof may be poor and humble, Gina; but it is home. And with all my heart I say: here dwells my happiness.

He begins to play again; almost immediately after, a knocking is heard at the entrance door.

GINA. (*Rising.*) Hush, Ekdal,—I think there's some one at the door.

HIALMAR. (*Laying the flute on the bookcase.*) There! Again!

GINA goes and opens the door.

GREGERS WERLE. (*In the passage.*) Excuse me—

GINA. (*Starting back slightly.*) Oh!

GREGERS.—does not Mr. Ekdal, the photographer, live here?

GINA. Yes, he does.

HIALMAR. (*Going towards the door.*) Gregers! You here after all? Well, come in then.

GREGERS. (*Coming in.*) I told you I would come and look you up.

HIALMAR. But this evening—? Have you left the party?

GREGERS. I have left both the party and my father's house.—Good evening, Mrs. Ekdal. I don't know whether you recognise me?

GINA. Oh yes; it's not difficult to know young Mr. Werle again.

GREGERS. No, I am like my mother; and no doubt you remember her.

HIALMAR. Left your father's house, did you say?

GREGERS. Yes, I have gone to a hotel.

HIALMAR. Indeed. Well, since you're here, take off your coat and sit down.

GREGERS. Thanks.

He takes off his overcoat. He is now dressed in a plain grey suit of a countrified cut.

HIALMAR. Here, on the sofa. Make yourself comfortable.

GREGERS seats himself on the sofa; HIALMAR takes a chair at the table.

GREGERS. (*Looking around him.*) So these are your quarters, Hialmar—this is your home.

HIALMAR. This is the studio, as you see—

GINA. But it's the largest of our rooms, so we generally sit here.

HIALMAR. We used to live in a better place; but this flat has one great advantage: there are such capital outer rooms

GINA. And we have a room on the other side of the passage that we can let.

GREGERS. (*To* HIALMAR.) Ah—so you have lodgers too?

HIALMAR. No, not yet. They're not so easy to find, you see; you have to keep your eyes open. (*To* HEDVIG.) What about that beer, eh?

HEDVIG *nods and goes out into the kitchen.*

GREGERS. So that is your daughter?

HIALMAR. Yes, that is Hedvig.

GREGERS. And she is your only child?

HIALMAR. Yes, the only one. She is the joy of our lives, and—(*lowering his voice.*)—at the same time our deepest sorrow, Gregers.

GREGERS. What do you mean?

HIALMAR. She is in serious danger of losing her eyesight.

GREGERS. Becoming blind?

HIALMAR. Yes. Only the first symptoms have appeared as yet, and she may not feel it much for some time. But the doctor has warned us. It is coming, inexorably.

GREGERS. What a terrible misfortune! How do you account for it?

HIALMAR. (*Sighs.*) Hereditary, no doubt.

GREGERS. (*Starting.*) Hereditary?

GINA. Ekdal's mother had weak eyes.

HIALMAR. Yes, so my father says; I can't remember her.

GREGERS. Poor child! And how does she take it?

HIALMAR. Oh, you can imagine we haven't the heart to tell her of it. She dreams of no danger. Gay and careless and chirping like a little bird, she flutters onward into a life of endless night. (*Overcome.*) Oh, it is cruelly hard on me, Gregers.

HEDVIG *brings a tray with beer and glasses, which she sets upon the table.*

HIALMAR. (*Stroking her hair.*) Thanks, thanks, Hedvig.

HEDVIG *puts her arm round his neck and whispers in his ear.*

HIALMAR. No, no bread and butter just now. (*Looks up.*) But perhaps you would like some, Gregers.

GREGERS. (*With a gesture of refusal.*) No, no thank you.

HIALMAR. (*Still melancholy.*) Well, you can bring in a little all the same. If you have a crust, that is all I want. And plenty of butter on it, mind.

HEDVIG *nods gaily and goes out into the kitchen again.*

GREGERS. (*Who has been following her with his eyes.*) She seems quite strong and healthy otherwise.

GINA. Yes. In other ways there's nothing amiss with her, thank goodness.

GREGERS. She promises to be very like you, Mrs. Ekdal. How old is she now?

GINA. Hedvig is close on fourteen; her birthday is the day after to-morrow.

GREGERS. She is pretty tall for her age, then.

GINA. Yes, she's shot up wonderful this last year.

GREGERS. It makes one realise one's own age to see these young people growing up.— How long is it now since you were married?

GINA. We've been married—let me see—just on fifteen years.

GREGERS. Is it so long as that?

GINA. (*Becomes attentive; looks at him.*) Yes, it is indeed.

HIALMAR. Yes, so it is. Fifteen years all but a few months. (*Changing his tone.*) They must have been long years for you, up at the works, Gregers.

GREGERS. They seemed long—while I was living them; now they are over, I hardly know how the time has gone.

OLD EKDAL *comes from his room without his pipe, but with his old-fashioned uniform cap on his head; his gait is somewhat unsteady.*

EKDAL. Come now, HIALMAR, let's sit down and have a good talk about this—h'm—what was it again?

HIALMAR. (*Going towards him.*) Father, we have a visitor here—Gregers Werle.—I don't know if you remember him.

EKDAL. (*Looking at GREGERS, who has risen.*) Werle? Is that the son? What does he want with me?

HIALMAR. Nothing; it's me he has come to see.

EKDAL. Oh! Then there's nothing wrong?

HIALMAR. No, no, of course not.

EKDAL. (*With a large gesture.*) Not that I'm afraid, you know; but—

GREGERS. (*Goes over to him.*) I bring you a greeting from your old hunting-grounds, Lieutenant Ekdal.

EKDAL. Hunting-grounds?

GREGERS. Yes, up in Höidal, about the works, you know.

EKDAL. Oh, up there. Yes, I knew all those places well in the old days.

GREGERS. You were a great sportsman then.

EKDAL. So I was, I don't deny it. You're looking at my uniform cap. I don't ask anybody's leave to wear it in the house. So long as I don't go out in the streets with it—

HEDVIG brings a plate of bread and butter, which she puts upon the table.

HIALMAR. Sit down, father, and have a glass of beer. Help yourself, Gregers.

EKDAL *mutters and stumbles over to the sofa.* GREGERS *seats himself on the chair nearest to him,* HIALMAR *on the other side of* GREGERS. GINA *sits a little way from the table, sewing;* HEDVIG *stands beside her father.*

GREGERS. Can you remember, Lieutenant Ekdal, how Hialmar and I used to come up and visit you in the summer and at Christmas?

EKDAL. Did you? No, no, no; I don't remember it. But sure enough I've been a tidy bit of a sportsman in my day. I've shot bears too. I've shot nine of 'em, no less.

GREGERS. (*Looking sympathetically at him.*) And now you never get any shooting?

EKDAL. Can't just say that, sir. Get a shot now and then perhaps. Of course not in the old way. For the woods you see—the woods, the woods—! (*Drinks.*) Are the woods fine up there now?

GREGERS. Not so fine as in your time. They have been thinned a good deal.

EKDAL. Thinned? (*More softly, and as if afraid.*) It's dangerous work that. Bad things come of it. The woods revenge themselves.

HIALMAR. (*Filling up his glass.*) Come—a little more, father.

GREGERS. How can a man like you—such a man for the open air—live in the midst of a stuffy town, boxed within four walls?

EKDAL. (*Laughs quietly and glances at* HIALMAR.) Oh, it's not so bad here. Not at all so bad.

GREGERS. But don't you miss all the things that used to be a part of your very being— the cool sweeping breezes, the free life in the woods and on the uplands, among beasts and birds—?

EKDAL. (*Smiling.*) HIALMAR, shall we let him see it?

HIALMAR. (*Hastily and a little embarrassed.*) Oh, no no, father; not this evening.

GREGERS. What does he want to show me?

HIALMAR. Oh, it's only something—you can see it another time.

GREGERS. (*Continues, to the old man.*) You see I have been thinking, Lieutenant Ekdal, that you should come up with me to the works; I am sure to be going back soon. No doubt you could get some copying there too. And here, you have nothing on earth to interest you—nothing to liven you up.

EKDAL. (*Stares in astonishment at him.*) Have I nothing on earth to—!

GREGERS. Of course you have Hialmar; but then he has his own family. And a man like you, who has always had such a passion for what is free and wild—

EKDAL. (*Thumps the table.*) Hialmar, he shall see it!

HIALMAR. Oh, do you think it's worth while, father? It's all dark.

EKDAL. Nonsense; it's moonlight. (*Rises.*) He shall see it, I tell you. Let me pass! Come and help me, Hialmar.

HEDVIG. Oh yes, do, father!

HIALMAR. (*Rising.*) Very well then.

GREGERS. (*To* GINA.) What is it?

GINA. Oh, nothing so very wonderful, after all.

> EKDAL *and* HIALMAR *have gone to the back wall and are each pushing back a side of the sliding door;* HEDVIG *helps the old man;* GREGERS *remains standing by the sofa;* GINA *sits still and sews. Through the open doorway a large, deep irregular garret is seen with odd nooks and corners; a couple of stove-pipes running through it, from rooms below. There are skylights through which clear moonbeams shine in on some parts of the great room; others lie in deep shadow.*

EKDAL. (*To* GREGERS.) You may come close up if you like.

GREGERS. (*Going over to them.*) Why, what is it?

EKDAL. Look for yourself. H'm.

HIALMAR. (*Somewhat embarrassed.*) This belongs to father, you understand.

GREGERS. (*At the door, looks into the garre*t.) Why, you keep poultry, Lieutenant Ekdal.

EKDAL. Should think we did keep poultry. They've gone to roost now. But you should just see our fowls by daylight, sir!

HEDVIG. And there's a—

EKDAL. Sh—sh! don't say anything about it yet.

GREGERS. And you have pigeons too, I see.

EKDAL. Oh yes, haven't we just got pigeons! They have their nest-boxes up there under the roof-tree; for pigeons like to roost high, you see.

HIALMAR. They aren't all common pigeons.

EKDAL. Common! Should think not indeed! We have tumblers, and a pair of pouters, too. But come here! Can you see that hutch down there by the wall?

GREGERS. Yes; what do you use it for?

EKDAL. That's where the rabbits sleep, sir.

GREGERS. Dear me; so you have rabbits too?

EKDAL. Yes, you may take my word for it, we have rabbits! He wants to know if we have rabbits, Hialmar! H'm! But now comes the thing, let me tell you! Here we have it! Move away, Hedvig. Stand here; that's right,—and now look down there.—Don't you see a basket with straw in it?

GREGERS. Yes. And I can see a fowl lying in the basket.

EKDAL. H'm—"a fowl"

GREGERS. Isn't it a duck?

EKDAL. (*Hurt.*) Why, of course it's a duck.

HIALMAR. But what kind of duck, do you think?

HEDVIG. It's not just a common duck—

EKDAL. Sh!

GREGERS. And it's not a Muscovy duck either.

EKDAL. No, Mr.—Werle; it's not a Muscovy duck; for it's a wild duck!

GREGERS. Is it really? A wild duck?

EKDAL. Yes, that's what it is. That "fowl" as you call it—is the wild duck. It's our wild duck, sir.

HEDVIG. My wild duck. It belongs to me.

GREGERS. And can it live up here in the garret? Does it thrive?

EKDAL. Of course it has a trough of water to splash about in, you know.

HIALMAR. Fresh water every other day.

GINA. (*Turning towards* HIALMAR.) But my dear Ekdal, it's getting icy cold here.

EKDAL. H'm, we had better shut up then. It's as well not to disturb their night's rest, too. Close up, Hedvig.

HIALMAR *and* HEDVIG *push the garret doors together.*

EKDAL. Another time you shall see her properly. (*Seats himself in the arm-chair by the stove.*) Oh, they're curious things, these wild ducks, I can tell you.

GREGERS. How did you manage to catch it, Lieutenant Ekdal?

EKDAL. I didn't catch it. There's a certain man in this town whom we have to thank for it.

GREGERS. (*Starts slightly.*) That man was not my father, was he?

EKDAL. You've hit it. Your father and no one else. H'm.

HIALMAR. Strange that you should guess that, Gregers.

GREGERS. You were telling me that you owed so many things to my father; and so I thought perhaps—

GINA. But we didn't get the duck from Mr. Werle himself—

EKDAL. It's Håkon Werle we have to thank for her, all the same, Gina. (*To* GREGERS.) He was shooting from a boat, you see, and he brought her down. But your father's sight is not very good now. H'm; she was only wounded.

GREGERS. Ah! She got a couple of slugs in her body, I suppose.

HIALMAR. Yes, two or three.

HEDVIG. She was hit under the wing, so that she couldn't fly.

GREGERS. And I suppose she dived to the bottom, eh?

EKDAL. (*Sleepily, in a thick voice.*) Of course. Always do that, wild ducks do. They shoot to the bottom as deep as they can get, sir—and bite themselves fast in the tangle and seaweed—and all the devil's own mess that grows down there. And they never come up again.

GREGERS. But your wild duck came up again, Lieutenant Ekdal.

EKDAL. He had such an amazingly clever dog, your father had. And that dog—he dived in after the duck and fetched her up again.

GREGERS. (*Who has turned to* HIALMAR.) And then she was sent to you here?

HIALMAR. Not at once; at first your father took her home. But she wouldn't thrive there; so Pettersen was told to put an end to her—

EKDAL. (*Half asleep.*) H'm—yes—Pettersen—that ass—

HIALMAR. (*Speaking more softly.*) That was how we got her, you see; for father knows Pettersen a little; and when he heard about the wild duck he got him to hand her over to us.

GREGERS. And now she thrives as well as possible in the garret there?

HIALMAR. Yes, wonderfully well. She has got fat. You see, she has lived in there so long now that she has forgotten her natural wild life; and it all depends on that.

GREGERS. You are right there, Hialmar. Be sure you never let her get a glimpse of the sky and the sea—. But I mustn't stay any longer; I think your father is asleep.

HIALMAR. Oh, as for that—

GREGERS. But, by-the-bye—you said you had a room to let—a spare room?

HIALMAR. Yes; what then? Do you know of anybody—?

GREGERS. Can I have that room?

HIALMAR. You?

GINA. Oh no, Mr. Werle, you—

GREGERS. May I have the room? If so, I'll take possession first thing to-morrow morning.

HIALMAR. Yes, with the greatest pleasure—

GINA. But, Mr. Werle, I'm sure it's not at all the sort of room for you.

HIALMAR. Why, Gina! how can you say that?

GINA. Why, because the room's neither large enough nor light enough, and—

GREGERS. That really doesn't matter, Mrs. Ekdal.

HIALMAR. I call it quite a nice room, and not at all badly furnished either.

GINA. But remember the pair of them underneath.

GREGERS. What pair?

GINA. Well, there's one as has been a tutor—

HIALMAR. That's Molvik—Mr. Molvik, B.A.

GINA. And then there's a doctor, by the name of Relling.

GREGERS. Relling? I know him a little; he practised for a time up in Höidal.

GINA. They're a regular rackety pair, they are. As often as not, they're out on the loose in the evenings; and then they come home at all hours, and they're not always just—

GREGERS. One soon gets used to that sort of thing. I daresay I shall be like the wild duck—

GINA. H'm; I think you ought to sleep upon it first, anyway.

GREGERS. You seem very unwilling to have me in the house, Mrs. Ekdal.

GINA. Oh, no! What makes you think that?

HIALMAR. Well, you really behave strangely about it,

GINA. (*To* GREGERS.) Then I suppose you intend to remain in the town for the present?

GREGERS. (*Putting on his overcoat.*) Yes, now I intend to remain here.

HIALMAR. And yet not at your father's? What do you propose to do, then?

GREGERS. Ah, if I only knew that, Hialmar, I shouldn't be so badly off! But when one has the misfortune to be called Gregers—! "Gregers"—and then "Werle" after it; did you ever hear anything so hideous?

HIALMAR. Oh, I don't think so at all.

GREGERS. Ugh! Bah! I feel I should like to spit upon the fellow that answers to such a name. But when a man is once for all doomed to be Gregers—Werle in this world, as I am—

HIALMAR. (*Laughs.*) Ha, ha! If you weren't Gregers Werle, what would you like to be?

GREGERS. If I should choose, I should like best to be a clever dog.

GINA. A dog!

HEDVIG. (*Involuntarily.*) Oh, no!

GREGERS. Yes, an amazingly clever dog; one that goes to the bottom after wild ducks when they dive and bite themselves fast in tangle and sea-weed, down among the ooze.

HIALMAR. Upon my word now, Gregers—I don't in the least know what you're driving at.

GREGERS. Oh, well, you might not be much the wiser if you did. It's understood, then, that I move in early to-morrow morning. (*To* GINA.) I won't give you any trouble; I do everything for myself. (*To* HIALMAR.) We can talk about the rest to-morrow.— Good-night, Mrs. EKDAL. (*Nods to* HEDVIG.) Good-night.

GINA. Good-night, Mr. Werle.

HEDVIG. Good-night.

HIALMAR. (*Who has lighted a candle.*) Wait a moment, I must show you a light; the stairs are sure to be dark.

GREGERS *and* HIALMAR *go out by the passage door.*

GINA. (*Looking straight before her, with her sewing in her lap.*) Wasn't that queer-like talk about wanting to be a dog?

HEDVIG. Do you know, mother—I believe he meant something quite different by that.

GINA. Why, what should he mean?

HEDVIG. Oh, I don't know; but it seemed to me he meant something different from what he said—all the time.

GINA. Do you think so? Yes, it was sort of queer.

HIALMAR. (*Comes back.*) The lamp was still burning. (*Puts out the candle and sets it down.*) Ah, now one can get a mouthful of food at last. (*Begins to eat the bread and butter.*) Well, you see, Gina—if only you keep your eyes open—

GINA. How, keep your eyes open—?

HIALMAR. Why, haven't we at last had the luck to get the room let? And just think—to a person like Gregers—a good old friend.

GINA. Well, I don't know what to say about it.

HEDVIG. Oh, mother, you'll see; it'll be such fun!

HIALMAR. You're very strange. You were so bent upon getting the room let before; and now you don't like it.

GINA. Yes I do, Ekdal; if it had only been to some one else—But what do you suppose Mr. Werle will say?

HIALMAR. Old Werle? It doesn't concern him.

GINA. But surely you can see that there's something amiss between them again, or the young man wouldn't be leaving home. You know very well those two can't get on with each other.

HIALMAR. Very likely not, but—

GINA. And now Mr. Werle may fancy it's you that has egged him on—

HIALMAR. Let him fancy so, then! Mr. Werle has done a great deal for me; far be it from me to deny it. But that doesn't make me everlastingly dependent upon him.

GINA. But, my dear Ekdal, maybe grandfather'll suffer for it. He may lose the little bit of work he gets from Gråberg.

HIALMAR. I could almost say: so much the better! Is it not humiliating for a man like me to see his grey-haired father treated as a pariah? But now I believe the fulness of time is at hand. (*Takes a fresh piece of bread and butter.*) As sure as I have a mission in life, I mean to fulfil it now!

HEDVIG. Oh, yes, father, do!

GINA. Hush! Don't wake him!

HIALMAR. (*More softly.*) I will fulfil it, I say. The day shall come when—And that is why I say it's a good thing we have let the room; for that makes me more independent, The man who has a mission in life must be independent. (*By the arm-chair, with emotion.*) Poor old white-haired father! Rely on your Hialmar. He has broad shoulders—strong shoulders, at any rate. You shall yet wake up some fine day and—(*To* GINA.) Do you not believe it?

GINA. (*Rising.*) Yes, of course I do; but in the meantime suppose we see about getting him to bed.

HIALMAR. Yes, come.

They take hold of the old man carefully.

ACT THREE.

HIALMAR EKDAL'S *studio. It is morning: the daylight shines through the large window in the slanting roof; the curtain is drawn back.*

HIALMAR *is sitting at the table, busy retouching a photograph; several others lie before him. Presently* GINA, *wearing her hat and cloak, enters by the passage door; she has a covered basket on her arm.*

HIALMAR. Back already, Gina?

GINA. Oh, yes, one can't let the grass grow under one's feet.

Sets her basket on a chair, and takes off her things.

HIALMAR. Did you look in at Gregers' room?

GINA. Yes, that I did. It's a rare sight, I can tell you; he's made a pretty mess to start off with.

HIALMAR. How so?

GINA. He was determined to do everything for himself, he said; so he sets to work to light the stove, and what must he do but screw down the damper till the whole room is full of smoke. Ugh! There was a smell fit to—

HIALMAR. Well, really!

GINA. But that's not the worst of it; for then he thinks he'll put out the fire, and goes and empties his water-jug into the stove, and so makes the whole floor one filthy puddle.

HIALMAR. How annoying!

GINA. I've got the porter's wife to clear up after him, pig that he is! But the room won't be fit to live in till the afternoon.

HIALMAR. What's he doing with himself in the meantime?

GINA. He said he was going out for a little while.

HIALMAR. I looked in upon him, too, for a moment—after you had gone.

GINA. So I heard. You've asked him to lunch.

HIALMAR. Just to a little bit of early lunch, you know. It's his first day—we can hardly do less. You've got something in the house, I suppose?

GINA. I shall have to find something or other.

HIALMAR. And don't cut it too fine, for I fancy Relling and Molvik are coming up, too. I just happened to meet Relling on the stairs, you see; so I had to—

GINA. Oh, are we to have those two as well?

HIALMAR. Good Lord—a couple more or less can't make any difference. Old Ekdal (*opens his door and looks in.*). I say, Hialmar—(*Sees* GINA.) Oh!

GINA. Do you want anything, grandfather?

EKDAL. Oh, no, it doesn't matter. H'm!

Retires again.

GINA. (*Takes up the basket.*) Be sure you see that he doesn't go out.

HIALMAR. All right, all right. And, Gina, a little herring-salad wouldn't be a bad idea; Relling and Molvik were out on the loose again last night.

GINA. If only they don't come before I'm ready for them—

HIALMAR. No, of course they won't; take your own time.

GINA. Very well; and meanwhile you can be working a bit.

HIALMAR. Well, I am working! I am working as hard as I can!

GINA. Then you'll have that job off your hands, you see.

She goes out to the kitchen with her basket. HIALMAR *sits for a time pencilling away at the photograph, in an indolent and listless manner.*

EKDAL. (*Peeps in, looks round the studio, and says softly.*): Are you busy?

HIALMAR. Yes, I'm toiling at these wretched pictures—

EKDAL. Well, well, never mind,—since you're so busy—h'm!

He goes out again; the door stands open.

HIALMAR. (*Continues for some time in silence then he lays down his brush and goes over to the door.*) Are you busy, father?

EKDAL. (*In a grumbling tone, within.*) If you're busy, I'm busy, too. H'm!

HIALMAR. Oh, very well, then.

Goes to his work again.

EKDAL. (*Presently, coming to the door again.*) H'm; I say, Hialmar, I'm not so very busy, you know.

HIALMAR. I thought you were writing.

EKDAL. Oh, devil take it! can't Gråberg wait a day or two? After all, it's not a matter of life and death.

HIALMAR. No; and you're not his slave either.

EKDAL. And about that other business in there—

HIALMAR. Just what I was thinking of. Do you want to go in? Shall I open the door for you?

EKDAL. Well, it wouldn't be a bad notion.

HIALMAR. (*Rises.*) Then we'd have that off our hands.

EKDAL. Yes, exactly. It's got to be ready first thing to-morrow. It is to-morrow, isn't it? H'm?

HIALMAR. Yes, of course it's to-morrow.

HIALMAR *and* EKDAL *push aside each his half of the sliding door. The morning sun is shining in through the skylights; some doves are flying about; others sit cooing, upon the perches; the hens are heard clucking now and then, further back in the garret.*

HIALMAR. There; now you can get to work, father.

EKDAL. (*Goes in.*) Aren't you coming, too?

HIALMAR. Well, really, do you know—; I almost think—(*Sees* GINA *at the kitchen door.*) I? No; I haven't time; I must work.—But now for our new contrivance—

He pulls a cord, a curtain slips down inside, the lower part consisting of a piece of old sailcloth, the upper part of a stretched fishing net. The floor of the garret is thus no longer visible.

HIALMAR. (*Goes to the table.*) So! Now, perhaps I can sit in peace for a little while.

GINA. Is he rampaging in there again?

HIALMAR. Would you rather have had him slip down to Madam Eriksen's? (*Seats himself.*) Do you want anything? You know you said—

GINA. I only wanted to ask if you think we can lay the table for lunch here?

HIALMAR. Yes; we have no early appointment, I suppose?

GINA. No, I expect no one to-day except those two sweethearts that are to be taken together.

HIALMAR. Why the deuce couldn't they be taken together another day!

GINA. Don't you know, I told them to come in the afternoon, when you are having your nap.

HIALMAR. Oh, that's capital. Very well, let us have lunch here then.

GINA. All right; but there's no hurry about laying the cloth; you can have the table for a good while yet.

HIALMAR. Do you think I am not sticking at my work? I'm at it as hard as I can!

GINA. Then you'll be free later on, you know.

Goes out into the kitchen again. Short pause.

EKDAL. (*In the garret doorway, behind the net.*) Hialmar!

HIALMAR. Well?

EKDAL. Afraid we shall have to move the water-trough, after all.

HIALMAR. What else have I been saying all along?

EKDAL. H'm—h'm—h'm.

Goes away from the door again. HIALMAR goes on working a little; glances towards the garret and half rises. HEDVIG comes in from the kitchen.

HIALMAR. (*Sits down again hurriedly.*) What do you want?

HEDVIG. I only wanted to come in beside you, father.

HIALMAR. (*After a pause.*). What makes you go prying around like that? Perhaps you are told off to watch me?

HEDVIG. No, no.

HIALMAR. What is your mother doing out there?

HEDVIG. Oh, mother's in the middle of making the herring-salad. (*Goes to the table*.). Isn't there any little thing I could help you with, father?

HIALMAR. Oh, no. It is right that I should bear the whole burden—so long as my strength holds out. Set your mind at rest, Hedvig; if only your father keeps his health—

HEDVIG. Oh, no, father! You mustn't talk in that horrid way.

She wanders about a little, stops by the doorway and looks into the garret.

HIALMAR. Tell me, what is he doing?

HEDVIG. I think he's making a new path to the water-trough.

HIALMAR. He can never manage that by himself! And here am I doomed to sit—!

HEDVIG. (*Goes to him*.) Let me take the brush, father; I can do it, quite well.

HIALMAR. Oh, nonsense; you will only hurt your eyes.

HEDVIG. Not a bit. Give me the brush.

HIALMAR. (*Rising*.) Well, it won't take more than a minute or two.

HEDVIG. Pooh, what harm can it do then? (*Takes the brush*.) There! (*Seats herself*.) I can begin upon this one.

HIALMAR. But mind you don't hurt your eyes! Do you hear? I won't be answerable; you do it on your own responsibility—understand that.

HEDVIG. (*Retouching*.) Yes, yes, I understand.

HIALMAR. You are quite clever at it, Hedvig. Only a minute or two, you know.

He slips through by the edge of the curtain into the garret. HEDVIG sits at her work. HIALMAR and EKDAL are heard disputing inside.

HIALMAR. (*Appears behind the net*.) I say, Hedvig—give me those pincers that are lying on the shelf. And the chisel. (*Turns away inside*.) Now you shall see, father. Just let me show you first what I mean!

HEDVIG has fetched the required tools from the shelf, and hands them to him through the net.

HIALMAR. Ah, thanks. I didn't come a moment too soon.

Goes back from the curtain again; they are heard carpentering and talking inside. HEDVIG stands looking in at them. A moment later there is a knock at the passage door; she does not notice it.

GREGERS WERLE. (*Bareheaded, in indoor dress, enters and stops near the door.*) H'm—!

HEDVIG. (*Turns and goes towards him.*) Good morning. Please come in.

GREGERS. Thank you. (*Looking towards the garret.*) You seem to have workpeople in the house.

HEDVIG. No, it is only father and grandfather. I'll tell them you are here.

GREGERS. No, no, don't do that; I would rather wait a little.

Seats himself on the sofa.

HEDVIG. It looks so untidy here—

Begins to clear away the photographs.

GREGERS. Oh, don't take them away. Are those prints that have to be finished off?

HEDVIG. Yes, they are a few I was helping father with.

GREGERS. Please don't let me disturb you.

HEDVIG. Oh, no.

She gathers the things to her and sits down to work; GREGERS looks at her, meanwhile, in silence.

GREGERS. Did the wild duck sleep well last night?

HEDVIG. Yes, I think so, thanks.

GREGERS. (*Turning towards the garret.*) It looks quite different by day from what it did last night in the moonlight.

HEDVIG. Yes, it changes ever so much. It looks different in the morning and in the afternoon; and it's different on rainy days from what it is in fine weather.

GREGERS. Have you noticed that?

HEDVIG. Yes, how could I help it?

GREGERS. Are you, too, fond of being in there with the wild duck?

HEDVIG. Yes, when I can manage it—

GREGERS. But I suppose you haven't much spare time; you go to school, no doubt.

HEDVIG. No, not now; father is afraid of my hurting my eyes.

GREGERS. Oh; then he reads with you himself?

HEDVIG. Father has promised to read with me; but he has never had time yet.

GREGERS. Then is there nobody else to give you a little help?

HEDVIG. Yes, there is Mr. Molvik; but he is not always exactly—quite—

GREGERS. Sober?

HEDVIG. Yes, I suppose that's it!

GREGERS. Why, then you must have any amount of time on your hands. And in there I suppose it is a sort world by itself?

HEDVIG. Oh, yes, quite. And there are such lots of wonderful things.

GREGERS. Indeed?

HEDVIG. Yes, there are big cupboards full of books; and a great many of the books have pictures in them.

GREGERS. Aha!

HEDVIG. And there's an old bureau with drawers and flaps, and a big clock with figures that go out and in. But the clock isn't going now.

GREGERS. So time has come to a standstill in there—in the wild duck's domain.

HEDVIG. Yes. And then there's an old paint-box and things of that sort; and all the books.

GREGERS. And you read the books, I suppose?

HEDVIG. Oh, yes, when I get the chance. Most of them are English though, and I don't understand English. But then I look at the pictures.—There is one great big book called "Harrison's History of London." [2] It must be a hundred years old; and there are such heaps of pictures in it. At the beginning there is Death with an hour-glass and a woman. I think that is horrid. But then there are all the other pictures of churches, and castles, and streets, and great ships sailing on the sea.

[2] *A New and Universal History of the Cities of London and Westminster*, by Walter Harrison. London, 1775, folio.

GREGERS. But tell me, where did all those wonderful things come from?

HEDVIG. Oh, an old sea captain once lived here, and he brought them home with him. They used to call him "The Flying Dutchman." That was curious, because he wasn't a Dutchman at all.

GREGERS. Was he not?

HEDVIG. No. But at last he was drowned at sea; and so he left all those things behind him.

GREGERS. Tell me now—when you are sitting in there looking at the pictures, don't you wish you could travel and see the real world for yourself?

HEDVIG. Oh, no! I mean always to stay at home and help father and mother.

GREGERS. To retouch photographs?

HEDVIG. No, not only that. I should love above everything to learn to engrave pictures like those in the English books.

GREGERS. H'm. What does your father say to that?

HEDVIG. I don't think father likes it; father is strange about such things. Only think, he talks of my learning basket-making, and straw-plaiting! But I don't think that would be much good.

GREGERS. Oh, no, I don't think so either.

HEDVIG. But father was right in saying that if I had learnt basket-making I could have made the new basket for the wild duck.

GREGERS. So you could; and it was you that ought to have done it, wasn't it?

HEDVIG. Yes, for it's my wild duck.

GREGERS. Of course it is.

HEDVIG. Yes, it belongs to me. But I lend it to father and grandfather as often as they please.

GREGERS. Indeed? What do they do with it?

HEDVIG. Oh, they look after it, and build places for it, and so on.

GREGERS. I see; for no doubt the wild duck is by far the most distinguished inhabitant of the garret?

HEDVIG. Yes, indeed she is; for she is a real wild fowl, you know. And then she is so much to be pitied; she has no one to care for, poor thing.

GREGERS. She has no family, as the rabbits have—

HEDVIG. No. The hens too, many of them, were chickens together; but she has been taken right away from all her friends. And then there is so much that is strange about the wild duck. Nobody knows her, and nobody knows where she came from either.

GREGERS. And she has been down in the depths of the sea.

HEDVIG. (*With a quick glance at him, represses a smile and asks.*): Why do you say "depths of the sea"?

GREGERS. What else should I say?

HEDVIG. You could say "the bottom of the sea."[3]

[3] GREGERS here uses the old-fashioned expression "havsens bund," while Hedvig would have him use the more commonplace "havens bund" or "havbunden."

GREGERS. Oh, mayn't I just as well say the depths of the sea?

HEDVIG. Yes; but it sounds so strange to me when other people speak of the depths of the sea.

GREGERS. Why so? Tell me why?

HEDVIG. No, I won't; it's so stupid.

GREGERS. Oh, no, I am sure it's not. Do tell me why you smiled.

HEDVIG. Well, this is the reason: whenever I come to realise suddenly—in a flash—what is in there, it always seems to me that the whole room and everything in it should be called "the depths of the sea." But that is so stupid.

GREGERS. You mustn't say that.

HEDVIG. Oh, yes, for you know it is only a garret.

GREGERS. (*Looks fixedly at her.*) Are you so sure of that?

HEDVIG. (*Astonished.*) That it's a garret?

56

GREGERS. Are you quite certain of it?

> HEDVIG *is silent, and looks at him open-mouthed.* GINA *comes in from the kitchen with the table things.*

GREGERS. (*Rising.*) I have come in upon you too early.

GINA. Oh, you must be somewhere; and we're nearly ready now, any way. Clear the table, Hedvig.

> HEDVIG *clears away her things; she and* GINA *lay the cloth during what follows.* GREGERS *seats himself in the arm-chair, and turns over an album.*

GREGERS. I hear you can retouch, Mrs. Ekdal.

GINA. (*With a side glance.*) Yes, I can.

GREGERS. That was exceedingly lucky.

GINA. How—lucky?

GREGERS. Since Ekdal took to photography, I mean.

HEDVIG. Mother can take photographs, too.

GINA. Oh, yes; I was bound to learn that.

GREGERS. So it is really you that carry on the business, I suppose?

GINA. Yes, when Ekdal hasn't time himself—

GREGERS. He is a great deal taken up with his old father, I daresay.

GINA. Yes; and then you can't expect a man like Ekdal to do nothing but take car-de-visits of Dick, Tom and Harry.

GREGERS. I quite agree with you; but having once gone in for the thing—

GINA. You can surely understand, Mr. Werle, that Ekdal's not like one of your common photographers.

GREGERS. Of course not; but still—

> *A shot is fired within the garret.*

GREGERS. (*Starting up.*) What's that?

GINA. Ugh! now they're firing again!

GREGERS. Have they firearms in there?

HEDVIG. They are out shooting.

GREGERS. What! (*At the door of the garret.*) Are you shooting, Hialmar?

HIALMAR. (*Inside the net.*) Are you there? I didn't know; I was so taken up—(*To* HEDVIG.) Why did you not let us know?

Comes into the studio.

GREGERS. Do you go shooting in the garret?

HIALMAR. (*Showing a double-barrelled pistol.*) Oh, only with this thing.

GINA. Yes, you and grandfather will do yourselves a mischief some day with that there pigstol.

HIALMAR. (*With irritation.*) I believe I have told you that this kind of firearm is called a pistol.

GINA. Oh, that doesn't make it much better, that I can see.

GREGERS. So you have become a sportsman, too, Hialmar?

HIALMAR. Only a little rabbit-shooting now and then. Mostly to please father, you understand.

GINA. Men are strange beings; they must always have something to pervert theirselves with.

HIALMAR. (*Snappishly.*) Just so; we must always have something to divert ourselves with.

GINA. Yes, that's just what I say.

HIALMAR. H'm. (*To* GREGERS.) You see the garret is fortunately so situated that no one can hear us shooting. (*Lays the pistol on the top shelf of the bookcase.*) Don't touch the pistol, Hedvig! One of the barrels is loaded; remember that.

GREGERS. (*Looking through the net.*) You have a fowling-piece too, I see.

HIALMAR. That is father's old gun. It's of no use now; something has gone wrong with the lock. But it's fun to have it all the same; for we can take it to pieces now and then, and clean and grease it, and screw it together again.—Of course, it's mostly father that fiddle-faddles with all that sort of thing.

HEDVIG. (*Beside GREGERS.*) Now you can see the wild duck properly.

GREGERS. I was just looking at her. One of her wings seems to me to droop a bit.

HEDVIG. Well, no wonder; her wing was broken, you know.

GREGERS. And she trails one foot a little. Isn't that so?

HIALMAR. Perhaps a very little bit.

HEDVIG. Yes, it was by that foot the dog took hold of her.

HIALMAR. But otherwise she hasn't the least thing the matter with her; and that is simply marvellous for a creature that has a charge of shot in her body, and has been between a dog's teeth—

GREGERS. (*With a glance at* HEDVIG.)—and.) that has lain in the depths of the sea— so long.

HEDVIG. (*Smiling.*) Yes.

GINA. (*Laying the table.*) That blessed wild duck! What a lot of fuss you do make over her.

HIALMAR. H'm;—will lunch soon be ready?

GINA. Yes, directly. Hedvig, you must come and help me now.

GINA *and* HEDVIG *go out into the kitchen.*

HIALMAR. (*In a low voice.*) I think you had better not stand there looking in at father; he doesn't like it. (GREGERS *moves away from the garret door.*) Besides, I may as well shut up before the others come. (*Claps his hands to drive the fowls back.*) Shh— shh, in with you! (*Draws up the curtain and pulls the doors together.*) All the contrivances are my own invention. It's really quite amusing to have things of this sort to potter with, and to put to rights when they get out of order. And it's absolutely necessary, too; for Gina objects to having rabbits and fowls in the studio.

GREGERS. To be sure; and I suppose the studio is your wife's special department?

HIALMAR. As a rule, I leave the everyday details of business to her; for then I can take refuge in the parlour and give my mind to more important things.

GREGERS. What things may they be, Hialmar?

HIALMAR. I wonder you have not asked that question sooner. But perhaps you haven't heard of the invention?

GREGERS. The invention? No.

HIALMAR. Really? Have you not? Oh, no, out there in the wilds—

GREGERS. So you have invented something, have you?

HIALMAR. It is not quite completed yet; but I am working at it. You can easily imagine that when I resolved to devote myself to photography, it wasn't simply with the idea of taking likenesses of all sorts of commonplace people.

GREGERS. No; your wife was saying the same thing just now.

HIALMAR. I swore that if I consecrated my powers to this handicraft, I would so exalt it that it should become both an art and a science. And to that end I determined to make this great invention.

GREGERS. And what is the nature of the invention? What purpose does it serve?

HIALMAR. Oh, my dear fellow, you mustn't ask for details yet. It takes time, you see. And you must not think that my motive is vanity. It is not for my own sake that I am working. Oh, no; it is my life's mission that stands before me night and day.

GREGERS. What is your life's mission?

HIALMAR. Do you forget the old man with the silver hair?

GREGERS. Your poor father? Well, but what can you do for him?

HIALMAR. I can raise up his self-respect from the dead, by restoring the name of Ekdal to honour and dignity.

GREGERS. Then that is your life's mission?

HIALMAR. Yes. I will rescue the shipwrecked man. For shipwrecked he was, by the very first blast of the storm. Even while those terrible investigations were going on, he was no longer himself. That pistol there—the one we use to shoot rabbits with—has played its part in the tragedy of the house of Ekdal.

GREGERS. The pistol? Indeed?

HIALMAR. When the sentence of imprisonment was passed—he had the pistol in his hand—

GREGERS. Had he—?

HIALMAR. Yes; but he dared not use it. His courage failed him. So broken, so demoralised was he even then! Oh, can you understand it? He, a soldier; he, who had shot nine bears, and who was descended from two lieutenant-colonels—one after the other, of course. Can you understand it, Gregers?

GREGERS. Yes, I understand it well enough.

HIALMAR. I cannot. And once more the pistol played a part in the history of our house. When he had put on the grey clothes and was under lock and key—oh, that was a terrible time for me, I can tell you. I kept the blinds drawn down over both my windows. When I peeped out, I saw the sun shining as if nothing had happened. I could not understand it. I saw people going along the street, laughing and talking about indifferent things. I could not understand it. It seemed to me that the whole of existence must be at a standstill—as if under an eclipse.

GREGERS. I felt that, too, when my mother died.

HIALMAR. It was in such an hour that Hialmar Ekdal pointed the pistol at his own breast.

GREGERS. You, too, thought of—!

HIALMAR. Yes.

GREGERS. But you did not fire?

HIALMAR. No. At the decisive moment I won the victory over myself. I remained in life. But I can assure you it takes some courage to choose life under circumstances like those.

GREGERS. Well, that depends on how you look at it.

HIALMAR. Yes, indeed, it takes courage. But I am glad I was firm: for now I shall soon perfect my invention; and Dr. Relling thinks, as I do myself, that father may be allowed to wear his uniform again. I will demand that as my sole reward.

GREGERS. So that is what he meant about his uniform—?

HIALMAR. Yes, that is what he most yearns for. You can't think how my heart bleeds for him. Every time we celebrate any little family festival—Gina's and my wedding-day, or whatever it may be—in comes the old man in the lieutenant's uniform of happier days. But if he only hears a knock at the door—for he daren't show himself to strangers, you know—he hurries back to his room again as fast as his old legs can carry him. Oh, it's heart-rending for a son to see such things!

GREGERS. How long do you think it will take you to finish your invention?

HIALMAR. Come now, you mustn't expect me to enter into particulars like that. An invention is not a thing completely under one's own control. It depends largely on inspiration—on intuition—and it is almost impossible to predict when the inspiration may come.

GREGERS. But it's advancing?

HIALMAR. Yes, certainly, it is advancing. I turn it over in my mind every day; I am full of it. Every afternoon, when I have had my dinner, I shut myself up in the parlour, where I can ponder undisturbed. But I can't be goaded to it; it's not a bit of good; Relling says so, too.

GREGERS. And you don't think that all that business in the garret draws you off and distracts you too much?

HIALMAR. No, no, no; quite the contrary. You mustn't say that. I cannot be everlastingly absorbed in the same laborious train of thought. I must have something alongside of it to fill up the time of waiting. The inspiration, the intuition, you see—when it comes, it comes, and there's an end of it.

GREGERS. My dear Hialmar, I almost think you have something of the wild duck in you.

HIALMAR. Something of the wild duck? How do you mean?

GREGERS. You have dived down and bitten yourself fast in the undergrowth.

HIALMAR. Are you alluding to the well-nigh fatal shot that has broken my father's wing—and mine, too?

GREGERS. Not exactly to that. I don't say that your wing has been broken; but you have strayed into a poisonous marsh, Hialmar; an insidious disease has taken hold of you, and you have sunk down to die in the dark.

HIALMAR. I? To die in the dark? Look here, Gregers, you must really leave off talking such nonsense.

GREGERS. Don't be afraid; I shall find a way to help you up again. I, too, have a mission in life now; I found it yesterday.

HIALMAR. That's all very well; but you will please leave me out of it. I can assure you that—apart from my very natural melancholy, of course—I am as contented as any one can wish to be.

GREGERS. Your contentment is an effect of the marsh poison.

HIALMAR. Now, my dear Gregers, pray do not go on about disease and poison; I am not used to that sort of talk. In my house nobody ever speaks to me about unpleasant things.

GREGERS. Ah, that I can easily believe.

HIALMAR. It's not good for me, you see. And there are no marsh poisons here, as you express it. The poor photographer's roof is lowly, I know—and my circumstances are narrow. But I am an inventor, and I am the bread-winner of a family. That exalts me above my mean surroundings.—Ah, here comes lunch!

> GINA and HEDVIG *bring bottles of ale, a decanter of brandy, glasses, etc. At the same time*, RELLING *and* MOLVIK *enter from the passage; they are both without hat or overcoat.* MOLVIK *is dressed in black.*

GINA. (*Placing the things upon the table.*) Ah, you two have come in the nick of time.

RELLING. Molvik got it into his head that he could smell herring-salad, and then there was no holding him.—Good morning again, Ekdal.

HIALMAR. Gregers, let me introduce you to Mr. Molvik. Doctor—Oh, you know Relling, don't you?

GREGERS. Yes, slightly.

RELLING. Oh, Mr. Werle, junior! Yes, we two have had one or two little skirmishes up at the Höidal works. You've just moved in?

GREGERS. I moved in this morning.

RELLING. Molvik and I live right under you; so you haven't far to go for the doctor and the clergyman, if you should need anything in that line.

GREGERS. Thanks, it's not quite unlikely; for yesterday we were thirteen at table.

HIALMAR. Oh, come now, don't let us get upon unpleasant subjects again!

RELLING. You may make your mind easy, Ekdal; I'll be hanged if the finger of fate points to you.

HIALMAR. I should hope not, for the sake of my family. But let us sit down now, and eat and drink and be merry.

GREGERS. Shall we not wait for your father?

HIALMAR. No, his lunch will be taken in to him later. Come along!

The men seat themselves at table, and eat and drink. GINA *and* HEDVIG *go in and out and wait upon them.*

RELLING. Molvik was frightfully screwed yesterday, Mrs. Ekdal.

GINA. Really? Yesterday again?

RELLING. Didn't you hear him when I brought him home last night?

GINA. No, I can't say I did.

RELLING. That was a good thing, for Molvik was disgusting last night.

GINA. Is that true, Molvik?

MOLVIK. Let us draw a veil over last night's proceedings. That sort of thing is totally foreign to my better self.

RELLING. (*To* GREGERS.) It comes over him like a sort of possession, and then I have to go out on the loose with him. Mr. MOLVIK is daemonic, you see.

GREGERS. Daemonic?

RELLING. Molvik is daemonic, yes.

GREGERS. H'm.

RELLING. And daemonic natures are not made to walk straight through the world; they must meander a little now and then.—Well, so you still stick up there at those horrible grimy works?

GREGERS. I have stuck there until now.

RELLING. And did you ever manage to collect that claim you went about presenting?

GREGERS. Claim? (*Understands him.*) Ah, I see.

HIALMAR. Have you been presenting claims, Gregers?

GREGERS. Oh, nonsense.

RELLING. Faith, but he has, though! He went round to all the cotters' cabins presenting something he called "the claim of the ideal."

GREGERS. I was young then.

RELLING. You're right; you were very young. And as for the claim of the ideal—you never got it honoured while I was up there.

GREGERS. Nor since either.

RELLING. Ah, then you've learnt to knock a little discount off, I expect.

GREGERS. Never, when I have a true man to deal with.

HIALMAR. No, I should think not, indeed. A little butter, Gina.

RELLING. And a slice of bacon for Molvik.

MOLVIK. Ugh; not bacon!

A knock at the garret door.

HIALMAR. Open the door, Hedvig; father wants to come out.

HEDVIG *goes over and opens the door a little way;* EKDAL *enters with a fresh rabbit-skin; she closes the door after him.*

EKDAL. Good morning, gentlemen! Good sport to-day. Shot a big one.

HIALMAR. And you've gone and skinned it without waiting for me—!

EKDAL. Salted it, too. It's good tender meat, is rabbit; it's sweet; it tastes like sugar. Good appetite to you, gentlemen!

Goes into his room.

MOLVIK. (*Rising.*) Excuse me—; I can't—; I must get downstairs immediately—

RELLING. Drink some soda water, man!

MOLVIK. (*Hurrying away.*) Ugh—ugh!

Goes out by the passage door.

RELLING. (*To* HIALMAR.) Let us drain a glass to the old hunter.

HIALMAR. (*Clinks glasses with him.*) To the undaunted sportsman who has looked death in the face!

RELLING. To the grey-haired—(*Drinks.*) By-the-bye, is his hair grey or white?

HIALMAR. Something between the two, I fancy; for that matter, he has very few hairs left of any colour.

RELLING. Well, well, one can get through the world with a wig. After all, you are a happy man, Ekdal; you have your noble mission to labour for—

HIALMAR. And I do labour, I can tell you.

RELLING. And then you have your excellent wife, shuffling quietly in and out in her felt slippers, with that see-saw walk of hers, and making everything cosy and comfortable about you—

HIALMAR. Yes, Gina—(*nods to her.*)—you were a good helpmate on the path of life.

GINA. Oh, don't sit there cricketizing me.

RELLING. And your Hedvig, too, Ekdal!

HIALMAR. (*Affected.*) The child, yes! The child before everything! Hedvig, come here to me. (*Strokes her hair.*) What day is it to-morrow, eh?

HEDVIG. (*Shaking him.*) Oh, no, you're not to say anything, father.

HIALMAR. It cuts me to the heart when I think what a poor affair it will be; only a little festivity in the garret—

HEDVIG. Oh, but that's just what I like!

RELLING. Just you wait till the wonderful invention sees the light, Hedvig!

HIALMAR. Yes, indeed—then you shall see—! Hedvig, I have resolved to make your future secure. You shall live in comfort all your days. I will demand—something or other—on your behalf. That shall be the poor inventor's sole reward.

HEDVIG. (*Whispering, with her arms round his neck.*) Oh, you dear, kind father!

RELLING. (*To* GREGERS.) Come now, don't you find it pleasant, for once in a way, to sit at a well-spread table in a happy family circle?

HIALMAR. Ah, yes, I really prize these social hours.

GREGERS. For my part, I don't thrive in marsh vapours.

RELLING. Marsh vapours?

HIALMAR. Oh, don't begin with that stuff again!

GINA. Goodness knows there's no vapours in this house, Mr. Werle; I give the place a good airing every blessed day.

GREGERS. (*Leaves the table.*) No airing you can give will drive out the taint I mean.

HIALMAR. Taint!

GINA. Yes, what do you say to that, Ekdal!

RELLING. Excuse me—may it not be you yourself that have brought the taint from those mines up there?

GREGERS. It is like you to call what I bring into this house a taint.

RELLING. (*Goes up to him.*) Look here, Mr. Werle, junior: I have a strong suspicion that you are still carrying about that "claim of the ideal" large as life, in your coat-tail pocket.

GREGERS. I carry it in my breast.

RELLING. Well, wherever you carry it, I advise you not to come dunning us with it here, so long as I am on the premises.

GREGERS. And if I do so none the less?

RELLING. Then you'll go head-foremost down the stairs; now I've warned you.

HIALMAR. (*Rising.*) Oh, but Relling—!

GREGERS. Yes, you may turn me out—

GINA. (*Interposing between them.*) We can't have that,

RELLING. But I must say, Mr. Werle, it ill becomes you to talk about vapours and taints, after all the mess you made with your stove.

A knock at the passage door.

HEDVIG. Mother, there's somebody knocking.

HIALMAR. There now, we're going to have a whole lot of people!

GINA. I'll go (*Goes over and opens the door, starts, and draws back.*) Oh—oh, dear!

WERLE, *in a fur coat, advances one step into the room.*

WERLE. Excuse me; but I think my son is staying here.

GINA. (*With a gulp.*) Yes.

HIALMAR. (*Approaching him.*) Won't you do us the honour to—?

WERLE. Thank you, I merely wish to speak to my son.

GREGERS. What is it? Here I am.

WERLE. I want a few words with you, in your room.

GREGERS. In my room? Very well—(*About to go.*).

GINA. No, no, your room's not in a fit state—

WERLE. Well then, out in the passage here; I want to have a few words with you alone.

HIALMAR. You can have them here, sir. Come into the parlour, Relling.

> HIALMAR *and* RELLING *go off to the right.* GINA *takes* HEDVIG *with her into the kitchen.*

GREGERS. (*After a short pause.*) Well, now we are alone.

WERLE. From something you let fall last evening, and from your coming to lodge with the Ekdals, I can't help inferring that you intend to make yourself unpleasant to me, in one way or another.

GREGERS. I intend to open Hialmar Ekdal's eyes. He shall see his position as it really is—that is all.

WERLE. Is that the mission in life you spoke of yesterday?

GREGERS. Yes. You have left me no other.

WERLE. Is it I, then, that have crippled your mind, Gregers?

GREGERS. You have crippled my whole life. I am not thinking of all that about mother—But it's thanks to you that I am continually haunted and harassed by a guilty conscience.

WERLE. Indeed! It is your conscience that troubles you, is it?

GREGERS. I ought to have taken a stand against you when the trap was set for Lieutenant Ekdal. I ought to have cautioned him; for I had a misgiving as to what was in the wind.

WERLE. Yes, that was the time to have spoken.

GREGERS. I did not dare to, I was so cowed and spiritless. I was mortally afraid of you—not only then, but long afterwards.

WERLE. You have got over that fear now, it appears.

GREGERS. Yes, fortunately. The wrong done to old Ekdal, both by me and by—others, can never be undone; but Hialmar I can rescue from all the falsehood and deception that are bringing him to ruin.

WERLE. Do you think that will be doing him a kindness?

GREGERS. I have not the least doubt of it.

WERLE. You think our worthy photographer is the sort of man to appreciate such friendly offices?

GREGERS. Yes, I do.

WERLE. H'm—we shall see.

GREGERS. Besides, if I am to go on living, I must try to find some cure for my sick conscience.

WERLE. It will never be sound. Your conscience has been sickly from childhood. That is a legacy from your mother, Gregers—the only one she left you.

GREGERS. (*With a scornful half-smile.*) Have you not yet forgiven her for the mistake you made in supposing she would bring you a fortune?

WERLE. Don't let us wander from the point.—Then you hold to your purpose of setting young Ekdal upon what you imagine to be the right scent?

GREGERS. Yes, that is my fixed resolve.

WERLE. Well, in that case I might have spared myself this visit; for, of course, it is useless to ask whether you will return home with me?

GREGERS. Quite useless.

WERLE. And I suppose you won't enter the firm either?

GREGERS. No.

WERLE. Very good. But as I am thinking of marrying again, your share in the property will fall to you at once. [4]

[4] By Norwegian law, before a widower can marry again, a certain proportion of his property must be settled on his children by his former marriage.

GREGERS. (*Quickly.*) No, I do not want that.

WERLE. You don't want it?

GREGERS. No, I dare not take it, for conscience' sake.

WERLE. (*After a pause.*) Are you going up to the works again?

GREGERS. No; I consider myself released from your service.

WERLE. But what are you going to do?

GREGERS. Only to fulfil my mission; nothing more.

WERLE. Well but afterwards? What are you going to live upon?

GREGERS. I have laid by a little out of my salary.

WERLE. How long will that last?

GREGERS. I think it will last my time.

WERLE. What do you mean?

GREGERS. I shall answer no more questions.

WERLE. Good-bye then, Gregers.

GREGERS. Good-bye.

WERLE *goes.*

HIALMAR. (*Peeping in.*) He's gone, isn't he?

GREGERS. Yes.

HIALMAR *and* RELLING *enter; also* GINA *and* HEDVIG *from the kitchen.*

RELLING. That luncheon-party was a failure.

GREGERS. Put on your coat, Hialmar; I want you to come for a long walk with me.

HIALMAR. With pleasure. What was it your father wanted? Had it anything to do with me?

GREGERS. Come along. We must have a talk. I'll go and put on my overcoat.

Goes out by the passage door.

GINA. You shouldn't go out with him, Ekdal.

RELLING. No, don't you do it. Stay where you are.

HIALMAR. (*Gets his hat and overcoat.*) Oh, nonsense! When a friend of my youth feels impelled to open his mind to me in private—

RELLING. But devil take it—don't you see that the fellow's mad, cracked, demented!

GINA. There, what did I tell you! His mother before him had crazy fits like that sometimes.

HIALMAR. The more need for a friend's watchful eye. (*To* GINA.) Be sure you have dinner ready in good time. Good-bye for the present.

Goes out by the passage door.

RELLING. It's a thousand pities the fellow didn't go to hell through one of the Höidal mines.

GINA. Good Lord! what makes you say that?

RELLING. (*Muttering.*) Oh, I have my own reasons.

GINA. Do you think young Werle is really mad?

RELLING. No, worse luck; he's no madder than most other people. But one disease he has certainly got in his system.

GINA. What is it that's the matter with him?

RELLING. Well, I'll tell you, Mrs. Ekdal. He is suffering from an acute attack of integrity.

GINA. Integrity?

HEDVIG. Is that a kind of disease?

RELLING. Yes, it's a national disease; but it only appears sporadically. (*Nods to* GINA.) Thanks for your hospitality.
He goes out by the passage door.

GINA. (*Moving restlessly to and fro.*) Ugh, that Gregers Werle—he was always a wretched creature.

HEDVIG. (*Standing by the table, and looking searchingly at her.*) I think all this is very strange.

ACT FOUR.

HIALMAR EKDAL'S *studio. A photograph has just been taken; a camera with the cloth over it, a pedestal, two chairs, a folding table, etc., are standing out in the room. Afternoon light; the sun is going down; a little later it begins to grow dusk.*

GINA *stands in the passage doorway, with a little box and a wet glass plate in her hand, and is speaking to somebody outside.*

GINA. *Yes, certainly. When I make a promise I keep it. The first dozen shall be ready on Monday. Good afternoon.*

Someone is heard going downstairs. GINA *shuts the door, slips the plate into the box, and puts it into the covered camera.*

HEDVIG. (*Comes in from the kitchen.*) Are they gone?

GINA. (*Tidying up.*) Yes, thank goodness, I've got rid of them at last.

HEDVIG. But can you imagine why father hasn't come home yet?

GINA. Are you sure he's not down in Relling's room?

HEDVIG. No, he's not; I ran down the kitchen stair just now and asked.

GINA. And his dinner standing and getting cold, too.

HEDVIG. Yes, I can't understand it. Father's always so careful to be home to dinner!

GINA. Oh, he'll be here directly, you'll see.

HEDVIG. I wish he would come; everything seems so queer to-day.

GINA. (*Calls out.*) Here he is!

HIALMAR EKDAL *comes in at the passage door.*

HEDVIG. (*Going to him.*) Father! Oh, what a time we've been waiting for you!

GINA. (*Glancing sidelong at him.*) You've been out a long time, Ekdal.

HIALMAR. (*Without looking at her.*) Rather long, yes.

He takes off his overcoat; GINA *and* HEDVIG *go to help him; he motions them away.*

GINA. Perhaps you've had dinner with Werle?

HIALMAR. (*Hanging up his coat.*) No.

GINA. (*Going towards the kitchen door.*) Then I'll bring some in for you.

HIALMAR. No; let the dinner alone. I want nothing to eat.

HEDVIG. (*Going nearer to him.*) Are you not well, father?

HIALMAR. Well? Oh, yes, well enough. We have had a tiring walk, Gregers and I.

GINA. You didn't ought to have gone so far, Ekdal; you're not used to it.

HIALMAR. H'm; there's many a thing a man must get used to in this world. (*Wanders about the room.*) Has any one been here whilst I was out?

GINA. Nobody but the two sweethearts.

HIALMAR. No new orders?

GINA. No, not to-day.

HEDVIG. There will be some to-morrow, father, you'll see.

HIALMAR. I hope there will; for to-morrow I am going to set to work in real earnest.

HEDVIG. To-morrow! Don't you remember what day it is to-morrow?

HIALMAR. Oh, yes, by-the-bye—. Well, the day after, then. Henceforth I mean to do everything myself; I shall take all the work into my own hands.

GINA. Why, what can be the good of that, Ekdal? It'll only make your life a burden to you. I can manage the photography all right; and you can go on working at your invention.

HEDVIG. And think of the wild duck, father,—and all the hens and rabbits and—!

HIALMAR. Don't talk to me of all that trash! From to-morrow I will never set foot in the garret again.

HEDVIG. Oh, but father, you promised that we should have a little party—

HIALMAR. H'm, true. Well, then, from the day after to-morrow. I should almost like to wring that cursed wild duck's neck!

HEDVIG. (*Shrieks.*) The wild duck!

GINA. Well I never!

HEDVIG. (*Shaking him.*) Oh, no, father; you know it's my wild duck!

HIALMAR. That is why I don't do it. I haven't the heart to—for your sake, Hedvig. But in my inmost soul I feel that I ought to do it. I ought not to tolerate under my roof a creature that has been through those hands.

GINA. Why, good gracious, even if grandfather did get it from that poor creature, Pettersen—

HIALMAR. (*Wandering about.*) There are certain claims—what shall I call them?—let me say claims of the ideal—certain obligations, which a man cannot disregard without injury to his soul.

HEDVIG. (*Going after him.*) But think of the wild duck,—the poor wild duck!

HIALMAR. (*Stops.*) I tell you I will spare it—for your sake. Not a hair of its head shall be—I mean, it shall be spared. There are greater problems than that to be dealt with. But you should go out a little now, Hedvig, as usual; it is getting dusk enough for you now.

HEDVIG. No, I don't care about going out now.

HIALMAR. Yes, do; it seems to me your eyes are blinking a great deal; all these vapours in here are bad for you. The air is heavy under this roof.

HEDVIG. Very well, then, I'll run down the kitchen stair and go for a little walk. My cloak and hat?—oh, they're in my own room. Father—be sure you don't do the wild duck any harm whilst I'm out.

HIALMAR. Not a feather of its head shall be touched. (*Draws her to him.*) You and I, Hedvig—we two—! Well, go along.

HEDVIG *nods to her parents and goes out through the kitchen.*

HIALMAR. (*Walks about without looking up.*) Gina.

GINA. Yes?

HIALMAR. From to-morrow—or, say, from the day after to-morrow—I should like to keep the household account-book myself.

GINA. Do you want to keep the accounts too, now?

HIALMAR. Yes; or to check the receipts at any rate.

GINA. Lord help us! that's soon done.

HIALMAR. One would hardly think so; at any rate you seem to make the money go a very long way. (*Stops and looks at her.*) How do you manage it?

GINA. It's because me and Hedvig, we need so little.

HIALMAR. Is it the case that father is very liberally paid for the copying he does for Mr. Werle?

GINA. I don't know as he gets anything out of the way. I don't know the rates for that sort of work.

HIALMAR. Well, what does he get, about? Let me hear!

GINA. Oh, it varies; I daresay it'll come to about as much as he costs us, with a little pocket-money over.

HIALMAR. As much as he costs us! And you have never told me this before!

GINA. No, how could I tell you? It pleased you so much to think he got everything from you.

HIALMAR. And he gets it from Mr. Werle.

GINA. Oh, well, he has plenty and to spare, he has.

HIALMAR. Light the lamp for me, please!

GINA. (*Lighting the lamp.*) And, of course, we don't know as it's Mr. Werle himself; it may be Gråberg—

HIALMAR. Why attempt such an evasion?

GINA. I don't know; I only thought—

HIALMAR. H'm!

GINA. It wasn't me that got grandfather that copying. It was Bertha, when she used to come about us.

HIALMAR. It seems to me your voice is trembling.

GINA. (*Putting the lamp-shade on.*) Is it?

HIALMAR. And your hands are shaking, are they not?

GINA. (*Firmly.*) Come right out with it, Ekdal. What has he been saying about me?

HIALMAR. Is it true—can it be true that—that there was an—an understanding between you and Mr. Werle, while you were in service there?

GINA. That's not true. Not at that time. Mr. Werle did come after me, that's a fact. And his wife thought there was something in it, and then she made such a hocus-pocus and hurly-burly, and she hustled me and bustled me about so that I left her service.

HIALMAR. But afterwards, then?

GINA. Well, then I went home. And mother—well, she wasn't the woman you took her for, Ekdal; she kept on worrying and worrying at me about one thing and another—for Mr. Werle was a widower by that time.

HIALMAR. Well, and then?

GINA. I suppose you've got to know it. He gave me no peace until he'd had his way.

HIALMAR. (*Striking his hands together*.) And this is the mother of my child! How could you hide this from me?

GINA. Yes, it was wrong of me; I ought certainly to have told you long ago.

HIALMAR. You should have told me at the very first;—then I should have known the sort of woman you were.

GINA. But would you have married me all the same?

HIALMAR. How can you dream that I would?

GINA. That's just why I didn't dare tell you anything, then. For I'd come to care for you so much, you see; and I couldn't go and make myself utterly miserable—

HIALMAR. (*Walks about*.) And this is my Hedvig's mother. And to know that all I see before me—(*Kicks at a chair*.)—all that I call my home—I owe to a favoured predecessor! Oh, that scoundrel Werle!

GINA. Do you repent of the fourteen—the fifteen years we've lived together?

HIALMAR. (*Placing himself in front of her*.) Have you not every day, every hour, repented of the spider's-web of deceit you have spun around me? Answer me that! How could you help writhing with penitence and remorse?

GINA, Oh, my dear Ekdal, I've had all I could do to look after the house and get through the day's work—

HIALMAR. Then you never think of reviewing your past?

GINA. No; Heaven knows I'd almost forgotten those old stories.

HIALMAR. Oh, this dull, callous contentment! To me there is something revolting about it. Think of it—never so much as a twinge of remorse!

GINA. But tell me, Ekdal—what would have become of you if you hadn't had a wife like me?

HIALMAR. Like you—!

GINA. Yes; for you know I've always been a bit more practical and wide-awake than you. Of course I'm a year or two older.

HIALMAR. What would have become of me!

GINA. You'd got into all sorts of bad ways when first you met me; that you can't deny.

HIALMAR. "Bad ways" do you call them? Little do you know what a man goes through when he is in grief and despair—especially a man of my fiery temperament.

GINA. Well, well, that may be so. And I've no reason to crow over you, neither; for you turned a moral of a husband, that you did, as soon as ever you had a house and home of your own.—And now we'd got everything so nice and cosy about us; and me and Hedvig was just thinking we'd soon be able to let ourselves go a bit, in the way of both food and clothes.

HIALMAR. In the swamp of deceit, yes.

GINA. I wish to goodness that detestable thing had never set his foot inside our doors!

HIALMAR. And I, too, thought my home such a pleasant one. That was a delusion. Where shall I now find the elasticity of spirit to bring my invention into the world of reality? Perhaps it will die with me; and then it will be your past, Gina, that will have killed it.

GINA. (*Nearly crying.*) You mustn't say such things, Ekdal. Me, that has only wanted to do the best I could for you, all my days!

HIALMAR. I ask you, what becomes of the breadwinner's dream? When I used to lie in there on the sofa and brood over my invention, I had a clear enough presentiment that it would sap my vitality to the last drop. I felt even then that the day when I held the patent in my hand—that day—would bring my—release. And then it was my dream that you should live on after me, the dead inventor's well-to-do widow.

GINA. (*Drying her tears.*) No, you mustn't talk like that, Ekdal. May the Lord never let me see the day I am left a widow!

HIALMAR. Oh, the whole dream has vanished. It is all over now. All over!

GREGERS WERLE *opens the passage door cautiously and looks in.*

GREGERS. May I come in?

HIALMAR. Yes, come in.

GREGERS. (*Comes forward, his face beaming with satisfaction, and holds out both his hands to them.*) Well, dear friends—! (*Looks from one to the other, and whispers to HIALMAR.*) Have you not done it yet?

HIALMAR. (*Aloud.*) It is done.

GREGERS. It is?

HIALMAR. I have passed through the bitterest moments of my life.

GREGERS. But also, I trust, the most ennobling.

HIALMAR. Well, at any rate, we have got through it for the present.

GINA. God forgive you, Mr. Werle.

GREGERS. (*In great surprise.*) But I don't understand this.

HIALMAR. What don't you understand?

GREGERS. After so great a crisis—a crisis that is to be the starting-point of an entirely new life—of a communion founded on truth, and free from all taint of deception—

HIALMAR. Yes, yes, I know; I know that quite well.

GREGERS. I confidently expected, when I entered the room, to find the light of transfiguration shining upon me from both husband and wife. And now I see nothing but dulness, oppression, gloom—

GINA. Oh, is that it?

Takes off the lamp-shade.

GREGERS. You will not understand me, Mrs. Ekdal. Ah, well, you, I suppose, need time to—. But you, Hialmar? Surely you feel a new consecration after the great crisis.

HIALMAR. Yes, of course I do. That is—in a sort of way.

GREGERS. For surely nothing in the world can compare with the joy of forgiving one who has erred, and raising her up to oneself in love.

HIALMAR. Do you think a man can so easily throw off the bitter cup I have drained?

GREGERS. No, not a common man, perhaps. But a man like you—!

HIALMAR. Good God! I know that well enough. But you must keep me up to it, Gregers. It takes time, you know.

GREGERS. You have much of the wild duck in you, Hialmar.

RELLING *has come in at the passage door.*

RELLING. Oho! is the wild duck to the fore again?

HIALMAR. Yes; Mr. Werle's wing-broken victim.

RELLING. Mr. Werle's—? So it's him you are talking about?

HIALMAR. Him and—ourselves.

RELLING. (*In an undertone to* GREGERS.) May the devil fly away with you!

HIALMAR. What is that you are saying?

RELLING. Only uttering a heartfelt wish that this quacksalver would take himself off. If he stays here, he is quite equal to making an utter mess of life, for both of you.

GREGERS. These two will not make a mess of life, Mr. Relling. Of course I won't speak of Hialmar—him we know. But she, too, in her innermost heart, has certainly something loyal and sincere—

GINA. (*Almost crying.*) You might have let me alone for what I was, then.

RELLING. (*To* GREGERS.) Is it rude to ask what you really want in this house?

GREGERS. To lay the foundations of a true marriage.

RELLING. So you don't think Ekdal's marriage is good enough as it is?

GREGERS. No doubt it is as good a marriage as most others, worse luck. But a true marriage it has yet to become.

HIALMAR. You have never had eyes for the claims of the ideal, Relling.

RELLING. Rubbish, my boy!—but excuse me, Mr. Werle: how many—in round numbers—how many true marriages have you seen in the course of your life?

GREGERS. Scarcely a single one.

RELLING. Nor I either.

GREGERS. But I have seen innumerable marriages of the opposite kind. And it has been my fate to see at close quarters what ruin such a marriage can work in two human souls.

HIALMAR. A man's whole moral basis may give away beneath his feet; that is the terrible part of it.

RELLING. Well, I can't say I've ever been exactly married, so I don't pretend to speak with authority. But this I know, that the child enters into the marriage problem. And you must leave the child in peace.

HIALMAR. Oh—Hedvig! my poor Hedvig!

RELLING. Yes, you must be good enough to keep Hedvig outside of all this. You two are grown-up people; you are free, in God's name, to make what mess and muddle you please of your life. But you must deal cautiously with Hedvig, I tell you; else you may do her a great injury.

HIALMAR. An injury!

RELLING. Yes, or she may do herself an injury—and perhaps others, too.

GINA. How can you know that, Relling?

HIALMAR. Her sight is in no immediate danger, is it?

RELLING. I am not talking about her sight. Hedvig is at a critical age. She may be getting all sorts of mischief into her head.

GINA. That's true—I've noticed it already! She's taken to carrying on with the fire, out in the kitchen. She calls it playing at house-on-fire. I'm often scared for fear she really sets fire to the house.

RELLING. You see; I thought as much.

GREGERS. (*To* RELLING.) But how do you account for that?

RELLING. (*Sullenly.*) Her constitution's changing, sir.

HIALMAR. So long as the child has me—! So long as I am above ground—!

A knock at the door.

GINA. Hush, Ekdal; there's some one in the passage. (*Calls out.*) Come in!

MRS. SÖRBY, *in walking dress, comes in.*

MRS. SÖRBY. Good evening.

GINA. (*Going towards her.*) Is it really you, Bertha?

MRS. SÖRBY. Yes, of course it is. But I'm disturbing you, I'm afraid?

HIALMAR. No, not at all; an emissary from that house—

Mrs. Sörby. (*To* GINA.) To tell the truth, I hoped your men-folk would be out at this time. I just ran up to have a little chat with you, and to say good-bye.

GINA. Good-bye? Are you going away, then?

MRS. SÖRBY. Yes, to-morrow morning,—up to Höidal. Mr. Werle started this afternoon. (*Lightly to* GREGERS.) He asked me to say good-bye for him.

GINA. Only fancy—!

HIALMAR. So Mr. Werle has gone? And now you are going after him?

MRS. SÖRBY. Yes, what do you say to that, Ekdal?

HIALMAR. I say: beware!

GREGERS. I must explain the situation. My father and Mrs. Sörby are going to be married.

HIALMAR. Going to be married!

GINA. Oh, Bertha! So it's come to that at last!

RELLING. (*His voice quivering a little.*) This is surely not true?

MRS. SÖRBY. Yes, my dear Relling, it's true enough.

RELLING. You are going to marry again?

MRS. SÖRBY. Yes, it looks like it. Werle has got a special licence, and we are going to be married quite quietly, up at the works.

GREGERS. Then I must wish you all happiness, like a dutiful stepson.

MRS. SÖRBY. Thank you very much—if you mean what you say. I certainly hope it will lead to happiness, both for Werle and for me.

RELLING. You have every reason to hope that. Mr. Werle never gets drunk—so far as I know; and I don't suppose he's in the habit of thrashing his wives, like the late lamented horse-doctor.

MRS. SÖRBY. Come now, let Sörby rest in peace. He had his good points, too.

RELLING. Mr. Werle has better ones, I have no doubt.

MRS. SÖRBY. He hasn't frittered away all that was good in him, at any rate. The man who does that must take the consequences.

RELLING. I shall go out with Molvik this evening.

MRS. SÖRBY. You mustn't do that, Relling. Don't do it—for my sake.

RELLING. There's nothing else for it. (*To* HIALMAR.) If you're going with us, come along.

GINA. No, thank you. Ekdal doesn't go in for that sort of dissertation.

HIALMAR. (*Half aloud, in vexation.*) Oh, do hold your tongue!

RELLING. Good-bye, Mrs.—Werle.

Goes out through the passage door.

GREGERS. (*To* MRS. SÖRBY.) You seem to know Dr. Relling pretty intimately.

MRS. SÖRBY. Yes, we have known each other for many years. At one time it seemed as if things might have gone further between us.

GREGERS. It was surely lucky for you that they did not.

MRS. SÖRBY. You may well say that. But I have always been wary of acting on impulse. A woman can't afford absolutely to throw herself away.

GREGERS. Are you not in the least afraid that I may let my father know about this old friendship?

MRS. SÖRBY. Why, of course, I have told him all about it myself.

GREGERS. Indeed?

MRS. SÖRBY. Your father knows every single thing that can, with any truth, be said about me. I have told him all; it was the first thing I did when I saw what was in his mind.

GREGERS. Then you have been franker than most people, I think.

MRS. SÖRBY. I have always been frank. We women find that the best policy.

HIALMAR. What do you say to that, Gina?

GINA. Oh, we're not all alike, us women aren't. Some are made one way, some another.

MRS. SÖRBY. Well, for my part, Gina, I believe it's wisest to do as I've done. And Werle has no secrets either, on his side. That's really the great bond between us, you see. Now he can talk to me as openly as a child. He has never had the chance to do that before. Fancy a man like him, full of health and vigour, passing his whole youth and the best years of his life in listening to nothing but penitential sermons! And very often the sermons had for their text the most imaginary offences—at least so I understand.

GINA. That's true enough.

GREGERS. If you ladies are going to follow up this topic, I had better withdraw.

MRS. SÖRBY. You can stay as far as that's concerned. I shan't say a word more. But I wanted you to know that I had done nothing secretly or in an underhand way. I may seem to have come in for a great piece of luck; and so I have, in a sense. But after all, I don't think I am getting any more than I am giving. I shall stand by him always, and I can tend and care for him as no one else can, now that he is getting helpless.

HIALMAR. Getting helpless?

GREGERS. (*To* MRS. SÖRBY.) Hush, don't speak of that here.

MRS. SÖRBY. There is no disguising it any longer, however much he would like to. He is going blind.

HIALMAR. (*Starts.*) Going blind? That's strange. He, too, going blind!

GINA. Lots of people do.

MRS. SÖRBY. And you can imagine what that means to a business man. Well, I shall try as well as I can to make my eyes take the place of his. But I mustn't stay any longer; I have heaps of things to do.—Oh, by-the-bye, Ekdal, I was to tell you that if there is anything Werle can do for you, you must just apply to Gråberg.

GREGERS. That offer I am sure Hialmar Ekdal will decline with thanks.

MRS. SÖRBY. Indeed? I don't think he used to be so—

GINA. No, Bertha, Ekdal doesn't need anything from Mr. Werle now.

HIALMAR. (*Slowly, and with emphasis.*) Will you present my compliments to your future husband, and say that I intend very shortly to call upon Mr. Gråberg—

GREGERS. What! You don't really mean that?

HIALMAR. To call upon Mr. Gråberg, I say, and obtain an account of the sum I owe his principal. I will pay that debt of honour—ha ha ha! a debt of honour, let us call it! In any case, I will pay the whole with five per cent. interest.

GINA. But, my dear Ekdal, God knows we haven't got the money to do it.

HIALMAR. Be good enough to tell your future husband that I am working assiduously at my invention. Please tell him that what sustains me in this laborious task is the wish to free myself from a torturing burden of debt. That is my reason for proceeding with the invention. The entire profits shall be devoted to releasing me from my pecuniary obligations to your future husband.

MRS. SÖRBY. Something has happened here.

HIALMAR. Yes, you are right.

MRS. SÖRBY. Well, good-bye. I had something else to speak to you about, Gina; but it must keep till another time. Good-bye.

HIALMAR *and* GREGERS *bow silently.* GINA *follows* MRS. SÖRBY *to the door.*

HIALMAR. Not beyond the threshold, Gina!

MRS. SÖRBY *goes;* GINA *shuts the door after her.*

HIALMAR. There now, GREGERS; I have got that burden of debt off my mind.

GREGERS. You soon will, at all events.

HIALMAR. I think my attitude may be called correct.

GREGERS. You are the man I have always taken you for.

HIALMAR. In certain cases, it is impossible to disregard the claim of the ideal. Yet, as the breadwinner of a family, I cannot but writhe and groan under it. I can tell you it is no joke for a man without capital to attempt the repayment of a long-standing obligation, over which, so to speak, the dust of oblivion had gathered. But it cannot be helped: the Man in me demands his rights.

GREGERS. (*Laying his hand on* HIALMAR'S *shoulder.*) My dear Hialmar—was it not a good thing I came?

HIALMAR. Yes.

GREGERS. Are you not glad to have had your true position made clear to you?

HIALMAR. (*Somewhat impatiently.*) Yes, of course I am. But there is one thing that is revolting to my sense of justice.

GREGERS. And what is that?

HIALMAR. It is that—but I don't know, whether I ought to express myself so unreservedly about your father.

GREGERS. Say what you please, so far as I am concerned.

HIALMAR. Well, then, is it not exasperating to think that it is not I, but he, who will realise the true marriage?

GREGERS. How can you say such a thing?

HIALMAR. Because it is clearly the case. Isn't the marriage between your father and Mrs. Sörby founded upon complete confidence, upon entire and unreserved candour on both sides? They hide nothing from each other, they keep no secrets in the background; their relation is based, if I may put it so, on mutual confession and absolution.

GREGERS. Well, what then?

HIALMAR. Well, is not that the whole thing? Did you not yourself say that this was precisely the difficulty that had to be overcome in order to found a true marriage?

GREGERS. But this is a totally different matter, Hialmar. You surely don't compare either yourself or your wife with those two—? Oh, you understand me well enough.

HIALMAR. Say what you like, there is something in all this that hurts and offends my sense of justice. It really looks as if there were no just providence to rule the world.

GINA. Oh, no, Ekdal; for God's sake don't say such things.

GREGERS. H'm; don't let us get upon those questions.

HIALMAR. And yet, after all, I cannot but recognise the guiding finger of fate. He is going blind.

GINA. Oh, you can't be sure of that.

HIALMAR. There is no doubt about it. At all events there ought not to be; for in that very fact lies the righteous retribution. He has hoodwinked a confiding fellow creature in days gone by—

GREGERS. I fear he has hoodwinked many.

HIALMAR. And now comes inexorable, mysterious Fate, and demands Werle's own eyes.

GINA. Oh, how dare you say such dreadful things! You make me quite scared.

HIALMAR. It is profitable, now and then, to plunge deep into the night side of existence.

HEDVIG, *in her hat and cloak, comes in by the passage door. She is pleasurably excited and out of breath.*

GINA. Are you back already?

HEDVIG. Yes, I didn't care to go any farther. It was a good thing, too; for I've just met some one at the door.

HIALMAR. It must have been that Mrs. Sörby.

HEDVIG. Yes.

HIALMAR. (*Walks up and down.*) I hope you have seen her for the last time. Silence. Hedvig, discouraged, looks first at one and then at the other, trying to divine their frame of mind.

HEDVIG. (*Approaching, coaxingly.*) Father.

HIALMAR. Well—what is it, Hedvig?

HEDVIG. Mrs. Sörby had something with her for me,

HIALMAR. (*Stops.*) For you?

HEDVIG. Yes. Something for to-morrow.

GINA. Bertha has always given you some little thing on your birthday.

HIALMAR. What is it?

HEDVIG. Oh, you mustn't see it now. Mother is to give it to me to-morrow morning before I'm up.

HIALMAR. What is all this hocus-pocus that I am to be in the dark about!

HEDVIG. (*Quickly.*) Oh, no, you may see it if you like. It's a big letter.

Takes the letter out of her cloak pocket.

HIALMAR. A letter, too?

HEDVIG. Yes, it is only a letter. The rest will come afterwards, I suppose. But fancy—a letter! I've never had a letter before. And there's "Miss" written upon it. (*Reads.*) "Miss Hedvig Ekdal." Only fancy—that's me!

HIALMAR. Let me see that letter.

HEDVIG. (*Hands it to him.*) There it is.

HIALMAR. That is Mr. Werle's hand.

GINA. Are you sure of that, Ekdal?

HIALMAR. Look for yourself.

GINA. Oh, what do I know about such-like things?

HIALMAR. Hedvig, may I open the letter—and read it?

HEDVIG. Yes, of course you may, if you want to.

GINA. No, not to-night, Ekdal; it's to be kept till to-morrow.

HEDVIG. (*Softly.*) Oh, can't you let him read it! It's sure to be something good; and then father will be glad, and everything will be nice again.

HIALMAR. I may open it then?

HEDVIG. Yes, do, father. I'm so anxious to know what it is.

HIALMAR. Well and good. (*Opens the letter, takes out a paper, reads it through, and appears bewildered.*) What is this—!

GINA. What does it say?

HEDVIG. Oh, yes, father—tell us!

HIALMAR. Be quiet. (*Reads it through again; he has turned pale, but says with self-control:.*) It is a deed of gift, Hedvig.

HEDVIG. Is it? What sort of gift am I to have?

HIALMAR. Read for yourself.

HEDVIG *goes over and reads for a time by the lamp.*

HIALMAR. (*Half-aloud, clenching his hands.*) The eyes! The eyes—and then that letter!

HEDVIG. (*Leaves off reading.*) Yes, but it seems to me that it's grandfather that's to have it.

HIALMAR. (*Takes letter from her.*) Gina—can you understand this?

GINA. I know nothing whatever about it; tell me what's the matter.

HIALMAR. Mr. Werle writes to Hedvig that her old grandfather need not trouble himself any longer with the copying, but that he can henceforth draw on the office for a hundred crowns a month

GREGERS. Aha!

HEDVIG. A hundred crowns, mother! I read that.

GINA. What a good thing for grandfather!

HIALMAR.—a hundred crowns a month so long as he needs it—that means, of course, so long as he lives.

GINA. Well, so he's provided for, poor dear.

HIALMAR. But there is more to come. You didn't read that, Hedvig. Afterwards this gift is to pass on to you.

HEDVIG. To me! The whole of it?

HIALMAR. He says that the same amount is assured to you for the whole of your life. Do you hear that, Gina?

GINA. Yes, I hear.

HEDVIG. Fancy—all that money for me! (*Shakes him.*) Father, father, aren't you glad—?

HIALMAR. (*Eluding her.*) Glad! (*Walks about.*) Oh what vistas—what perspectives open up before me! It is Hedvig, Hedvig that he showers these benefactions upon!

GINA. Yes, because it's Hedvig's birthday—

HEDVIG. And you'll get it all the same, father! You know quite well I shall give all the money to you and mother.

HIALMAR. To mother, yes! There we have it.

GREGERS. Hialmar, this is a trap he is setting for you.

HIALMAR. Do you think it's another trap?

GREGERS. When he was here this morning he said: Hialmar Ekdal is not the man you imagine him to be.

HIALMAR. Not the man—!

GREGERS. That you shall see, he said.

HIALMAR. He meant you should see that I would let myself be bought off—!

HEDVIG. Oh mother, what does all this mean?

GINA. Go and take off your things.

HEDVIG *goes out by the kitchen door, half-crying.*

GREGERS. Yes, Hialmar—now is the time to show who was right, he or I.

HIALMAR. (*Slowly tears the paper across, lays both pieces on the table, and says.*): Here is my answer.

GREGERS. Just what I expected.

HIALMAR. (*Goes over to* GINA, *who stands by the stove, and says in a low voice.*): Now please make a clean breast of it. If the connection between you and him was quite over when you—came to care for me, as you call it—why did he place us in a position to marry?

GINA. I suppose he thought as he could come and go in our house.

HIALMAR. Only that? Was not he afraid of a possible contingency?

GINA. I don't know what you mean.

HIALMAR. I want to know whether—your child has the right to live under my roof.

GINA. (*Draws herself up; her eyes flash.*) You ask that!

HIALMAR. You shall answer me this one question: Does Hedvig belong to me—or—? Well!

GINA. (*Looking at him with cold defiance.*) I don't know.

HIALMAR. (*Quivering a little.*) You don't know!

GINA. How should I know. A creature like me—

HIALMAR. (*Quietly turning away from her.*) Then I have nothing more to do in this house.

GREGERS. Take care, Hialmar! Think what you are doing!

HIALMAR. (*Puts on his overcoat.*) In this case, there is nothing for a man like me to think twice about.

GREGERS. Yes indeed, there are endless things to be considered. You three must be together if you are to attain the true frame of mind for self-sacrifice and forgiveness.

HIALMAR. I don't want to attain it. Never, never! My hat! (*Takes his hat.*) My home has fallen in ruins about me. (*Bursts into tears.*) Gregers, I have no child!

HEDVIG. (*Who has opened the kitchen door.*) What is that you're saying? (*Coming to him.*) Father, father!

GINA. There, you see!

HIALMAR. Don't come near me, Hedvig! Keep far away. I cannot bear to see you. Oh! those eyes—! Good-bye.

Makes for the door.

HEDVIG. (*Clinging close to him and screaming loudly.*) No! no! Don't leave me!

GINA. (*Cries out.*) Look at the child, Ekdal! Look at the child!

HIALMAR. I will not! I cannot! I must get out—away from all this!

He tears himself away from HEDVIG, *and goes out by the passage door.*

HEDVIG. (*With despairing eyes.*) He is going away from us, mother! He is going away from us! He will never come back again!

GINA. Don't cry, Hedvig. Father's sure to come back again.

HEDVIG. (*Throws herself sobbing on the sofa.*) No, no, he'll never come home to us any more.

GREGERS. Do you believe I meant all for the best, Mrs. Ekdal?

GINA. Yes, I daresay you did; but God forgive you, all the same.

HEDVIG. (*Lying on the sofa.*) Oh, this will kill me! What have I done to him? Mother, you must fetch him home again!

GINA. Yes yes yes; only be quiet, and I'll go out and look for him. (*Puts on her outdoor things.*) Perhaps he's gone in to Relling's. But you mustn't lie there and cry. Promise me!

HEDVIG. (*Weeping convulsively.*) Yes, I'll stop, I'll stop; if only father comes back!

GREGERS. (*To* GINA, *who is going.*) After all, had you not better leave him to fight out his bitter fight to the end?

GINA. Oh, he can do that afterwards. First of all, we must get the child quieted.

Goes out by the passage door.

HEDVIG. (*sits up and dries her tears.*) Now you must tell me what all this means. Why doesn't father want me any more?

GREGERS. You mustn't ask that till you are a big girl—quite grown-up.

HEDVIG. (*Sobs.*) But I can't go on being as miserable as this till I'm grown-up.—I think I know what it is.—Perhaps I'm not really father's child.

GREGERS. (*Uneasily.*) How could that be?

HEDVIG. Mother might have found me. And perhaps father has just got to know it; I've read of such things.

GREGERS. Well, but if it were so—

HEDVIG. I think he might be just as fond of me for all that. Yes, fonder almost. We got the wild duck in a present, you know, and I love it so dearly all the same.

GREGERS. (*Turning the conversation.*) Ah, the wild duck, by-the-bye! Let us talk about the wild duck a little, Hedvig.

HEDVIG. The poor wild duck! He doesn't want to see it any more either. Only think, he wanted to wring its neck!

GREGERS. Oh, he won't do that.

HEDVIG. No; but he said he would like to. And I think it was horrid of father to say it; for I pray for the wild duck every night, and ask that it may be preserved from death and all that is evil.

GREGERS. (*Looking at her.*) Do you say your prayers every night?

HEDVIG. Yes.

GREGERS. Who taught you to do that?

HEDVIG. I myself; one time when father was very ill, and had leeches on his neck, and said that death was staring him in the face.

GREGERS. Well?

HEDVIG. Then I prayed for him as I lay in bed; and since then I have always kept it up.

GREGERS. And now you pray for the wild duck too?

HEDVIG. I thought it was best to bring in the wild duck; for she was so weakly at first.

GREGERS. Do you pray in the morning, too?

HEDVIG. No, of course not.

GREGERS. Why not in the morning as well?

HEDVIG. In the morning it's light, you know, and there's nothing in particular to be afraid of.

GREGERS. And your father was going to wring the neck of the wild duck that you love so dearly?

HEDVIG. No; he said he ought to wring its neck, but he would spare it for my sake; and that was kind of father.

GREGERS. (*Coming a little nearer.*) But suppose you were to sacrifice the wild duck of your own free will for his sake.

HEDVIG. (*Rising.*) The wild duck!

GREGERS. Suppose you were to make a free-will offering, for his sake, of the dearest treasure you have in the world!

HEDVIG. Do you think that would do any good?

GREGERS. Try it, Hedvig.

HEDVIG. (*Softly, with flashing eyes.*) Yes, I will try it.

GREGERS. Have you really the courage for it, do you think?

HEDVIG. I'll ask grandfather to shoot the wild duck for me.

GREGERS. Yes, do.—But not a word to your mother about it.

HEDVIG. Why not?

GREGERS. She doesn't understand us.

HEDVIG. The wild duck! I'll try it to-morrow morning.

GINA *comes in by the passage door.*

HEDVIG. (*Going towards her.*) Did you find him, mother?

GINA. No, but I heard as he had called and taken Relling with him.

GREGERS. Are you sure of that?

GINA. Yes, the porter's wife said so. Molvik went with them, too, she said.

GREGERS. This evening, when his mind so sorely needs to wrestle in solitude—!

GINA. (*Takes off her things.*) Yes, men are strange creatures, so they are. The Lord only knows where Relling has dragged him to! I ran over to Madam Eriksen's, but they weren't there.

HEDVIG. (*Struggling to keep back her tears.*) Oh, if he should never come home any more!

GREGERS. He will come home again. I shall have news to give him to-morrow; and then you shall see how he comes home. You may rely upon that, Hedvig, and sleep in peace. Good-night.

He goes out by the passage door.

HEDVIG. (*Throws herself sobbing on* GINA'S *neck.*) Mother, mother!

GINA. (*Pats her shoulder and sighs.*) Ah yes; Relling was right, he was. That's what comes of it when crazy creatures go about presenting the claims of the—what-you-may-call-it.

ACT FIVE.

HIALMAR EKDAL'S *studio. Cold, grey morning light. Wet snow lies upon the large panes of the sloping roof-window.*

GINA *comes from the kitchen with an apron and bib on, and carrying a dusting-brush and a duster; she goes towards the sitting-room door. At the same moment* HEDVIG *comes hurriedly in from the passage.*

GINA. (*Stops.*) Well?

HEDVIG. Oh, mother, I almost think he's down at Relling's—

GINA. There, you see!

HEDVIG.—because the porter's wife says she could hear that Relling had two people with him when he came home last night.

GINA. That's just what I thought.

HEDVIG. But it's no use his being there, if he won't come up to us.

GINA. I'll go down and speak to him at all events.

OLD EKDAL, *in dressing-gown and slippers, and with a lighted pipe, appears at the door of his room.*

EKDAL. Hialmar—Isn't Hialmar at home?

GINA. No, he's gone out.

EKDAL. So early? And in such a tearing snowstorm? Well well; just as he pleases; I can take my morning walk alone.

He slides the garret door aside; HEDVIG *helps him; he goes in; she closes it after him.*

HEDVIG. (*In an undertone.*) Only think, mother, when poor grandfather hears that father is going to leave us.

GINA. Oh, nonsense; grandfather mustn't hear anything about it. It was a heaven's mercy he wasn't at home yesterday in all that hurly-burly.

HEDVIG. Yes, but—

GREGERS *comes in by the passage door.*

GREGERS. Well, have you any news of him?

GINA. They say he's down at Relling's.

GREGERS. At Relling's! Has he really been out with those creatures?

GINA. Yes, like enough.

GREGERS. When he ought to have been yearning for solitude, to collect and clear his thoughts—

GINA. Yes, you may well say so.

    RELLING *enters from the passage.*

HEDVIG. (*Going to him.*) Is father in your room?

GINA. (*At the same time.*) Is he there?

RELLING. Yes, to be sure he is.

HEDVIG. And you never let us know!

RELLING. Yes; I'm a brute. But in the first place I had to look after the other brute; I mean our daemonic friend, of course; and then I fell so dead asleep that—

GINA. What does Ekdal say to-day?

RELLING. He says nothing whatever.

HEDVIG. Doesn't he speak?

RELLING. Not a blessed word.

GREGERS. No no; I can understand that very well.

GINA. But what's he doing then?

RELLING. He's lying on the sofa, snoring.

GINA. Oh is he? Yes, Ekdal's a rare one to snore.

HEDVIG. Asleep? Can he sleep?

RELLING. Well, it certainly looks like it.

GREGERS. No wonder, after the spiritual conflict that has rent him—

GINA. And then he's never been used to gadding about out of doors at night.

HEDVIG. Perhaps it's a good thing that he's getting sleep, mother.

GINA. Of course it is; and we must take care we don't wake him up too early. Thank you, Relling. I must get the house cleaned up a bit now, and then—Come and help me, Hedvig.

GINA *and* HEDVIG *go into the sitting-room.*

GREGERS. (*Turning to* RELLING.) What is your explanation of the spiritual tumult that is now going on in Hialmar Ekdal?

RELLING. Devil a bit of a spiritual tumult have I noticed in him.

GREGERS. What! Not at such a crisis, when his whole life has been placed on a new foundation—? How can you think that such an individuality as Hialmar's—?

RELLING. Oh, individuality—he! If he ever had any tendency to the abnormal developments you call individuality, I can assure you it was rooted out of him while he was still in his teens.

GREGERS. That would be strange indeed,—considering the loving care with which he was brought up.

RELLING. By those two high-flown, hysterical maiden aunts, you mean?

GREGERS. Let me tell you that they were women who never forgot the claim of the ideal—but of course you will only jeer at me again.

RELLING. No, I'm in no humour for that. I know all about those ladies; for he has ladled out no end of rhetoric on the subject of his "two soul-mothers." But I don't think he has much to thank them for. Ekdal's misfortune is that in his own circle he has always been looked upon as a shining light—

GREGERS. Not without reason, surely. Look at the depth of his mind!

RELLING. I have never discovered it. That his father believed in it I don't so much wonder; the old lieutenant has been an ass all his days.

GREGERS. He has had a child-like mind all his days; that is what you cannot understand.

RELLING. Well, so be it. But then, when our dear, sweet Hialmar went to college, he at once passed for the great light of the future amongst his comrades too. He was handsome, the rascal—red and white—a shop-girl's dream of manly beauty; and with his superficially emotional temperament, and his sympathetic voice, and his talent for declaiming other people's verses and other people's thoughts—

GREGERS. (*Indignantly.*) Is it Hialmar Ekdal you are talking about in this strain?

RELLING. Yes, with your permission; I am simply giving you an inside view of the idol you are grovelling before.

GREGERS. I should hardly have thought I was quite stone blind.

RELLING. Yes you are—or not far from it. You are a sick man, too, you see.

GREGERS. You are right there.

RELLING. Yes. Yours is a complicated case. First of all, there is that plaguy integrity-fever; and then—what's worse—you are always in a delirium of hero-worship; you must always have something to adore, outside yourself.

GREGERS. Yes, I must certainly seek it outside myself.

RELLING. But you make such shocking mistakes about every new phoenix you think you have discovered. Here again you have come to a cotter's cabin with your claim of the ideal; and the people of the house are insolvent.

GREGERS. If you don't think better than that of Hialmar Ekdal, what pleasure can you find in being everlastingly with him?

RELLING. Well, you see, I'm supposed to be a sort of a doctor—save the mark! I can't but give a hand to the poor sick folk who live under the same roof with me.

GREGERS. Oh, indeed! Hialmar Ekdal is sick too, is he!

RELLING. Most people are, worse luck.

GREGERS. And what remedy are you applying in Hialmar's case?

RELLING. My usual one. I am cultivating the life-illusion [5] in him.

[5] "Livslögnen," literally "the life-lie."

GREGERS. Life-illusion? I didn't catch what you said.

RELLING. Yes, I said illusion. For illusion, you know, is the stimulating principle.

GREGERS. May I ask with what illusion Hialmar is inoculated?

RELLING. No, thank you; I don't betray professional secrets to quacksalvers. You would probably go and muddle his case still more than you have already. But my method is infallible. I have applied it to Molvik as well. I have made him "daemonic." That's the blister I have to put on his neck.

GREGERS. Is he not really daemonic then?

RELLING. What the devil do you mean by daemonic! It's only a piece of gibberish I've invented to keep up a spark of life in him. But for that, the poor harmless creature would have succumbed to self-contempt and despair many a long year ago. And then the old lieutenant! But he has hit upon his own cure, you see.

GREGERS. Lieutenant Ekdal? What of him?

RELLING. Just think of the old bear-hunter shutting himself up in that dark garret to shoot rabbits! I tell you there is not a happier sportsman in the world than that old man pottering about in there among all that rubbish. The four or five withered Christmas-trees he has saved up are the same to him as the whole great fresh Höidal forest; the cock and the hens are big game-birds in the fir-tops; and the rabbits that flop about the garret floor are the bears he has to battle with—the mighty hunter of the mountains!

GREGERS. Poor unfortunate old man! Yes; he has indeed had to narrow the ideals of his youth.

RELLING. While I think of it, Mr. Werle, junior—don't use that foreign word: ideals. We have the excellent native word: lies.

GREGERS. Do you think the two things are related?

RELLING. Yes, just about as closely as typhus and putrid fever.

GREGERS. Dr. Relling, I shall not give up the struggle until I have rescued Hialmar from your clutches!

RELLING. So much the worse for him. Rob the average man of his life-illusion, and you rob him of his happiness at the same stroke. (*To* HEDVIG, *who comes in from the sitting-room.*) Well, little wild-duck-mother, I'm just going down to see whether papa is still lying meditating upon that wonderful invention of his.

Goes out by passage door.

GREGERS. (*Approaches* HEDVIG.) I can see by your face that you have not yet done it.

HEDVIG. What? Oh, that about the wild duck! No.

GREGERS. I suppose your courage failed when the time came.

HEDVIG. No, that wasn't it. But when I awoke this morning and remembered what we had been talking about, it seemed so strange.

GREGERS. Strange?

HEDVIG. Yes, I don't know—Yesterday evening, at the moment, I thought there was something so delightful about it; but since I have slept and thought of it again, it somehow doesn't seem worth while.

GREGERS. Ah, I thought you could not have grown up quite unharmed in this house.

HEDVIG. I don't care about that, if only father would come up—

GREGERS. Oh, if only your eyes had been opened to that which gives life its value—if you possessed the true, joyous, fearless spirit of sacrifice, you would soon see how he would come up to you.—But I believe in you still, Hedvig. (*He goes out by the passage door.*)

> HEDVIG *wanders about the room for a time; she is on the point of going into the kitchen when a knock is heard at the garret door.* HEDVIG *goes over and opens it a little;* OLD EKDAL *comes out; she pushes the door to again.*

EKDAL. H'm, it's not much fun to take one's morning walk alone.

HEDVIG. Wouldn't you like to go shooting, grandfather?

EKDAL. It's not the weather for it to-day. It's so dark there, you can scarcely see where you're going.

HEDVIG. Do you never want to shoot anything besides the rabbits?

EKDAL. Do you think the rabbits aren't good enough?

HEDVIG. Yes, but what about the wild duck?

EKDAL. Ho-ho! are you afraid I shall shoot your wild duck? Never in the world. Never.

HEDVIG. No, I suppose you couldn't; they say it's very difficult to shoot wild ducks.

EKDAL. Couldn't! Should rather think I could.

HEDVIG. How would you set about it, grandfather?—I don't mean with my wild duck, but with others?

EKDAL. I should take care to shoot them in the breast, you know; that's the surest place. And then you must shoot against the feathers, you see—not the way of the feathers.

HEDVIG. Do they die then, grandfather?

EKDAL. Yes, they die right enough—when you shoot properly.—Well, I must go and brush up a bit. H'm—understand—h'm.

Goes into his room.

HEDVIG *waits a little, glances towards the sitting-room door, goes over to the book-case, stands on tip-toe, takes the double-barrelled pistol down from the shelf, and looks at it. GINA, with brush and duster, comes from the sitting-room. HEDVIG hastily lays down the pistol, unobserved.*

GINA. Don't stand raking amongst father's things, Hedvig.

HEDVIG. (*Goes away from the bookcase.*) I was only going to tidy up a little.

GINA. You'd better go into the kitchen, and see if the coffee's keeping hot; I'll take his breakfast on a tray, when I go down to him.

HEDVIG *goes out. GINA begins to sweep and clean up the studio. Presently the passage door is opened with hesitation, and HIALMAR EKDAL looks in. He has on his overcoat, but not his hat; he is unwashed, and his hair is dishevelled and unkempt. His eyes are dull and heavy.*

GINA. (*Standing with the brush in her hand, and looking at him.*) Oh, there now, Ekdal—so you've come after all?

HIALMAR. (*Comes in and answers in a toneless voice.*) I come only to depart again immediately.

GINA. Yes, yes, I suppose so. But, Lord help us! what a sight you are!

HIALMAR. A sight?

GINA. And your nice winter coat too! Well, that's done for.

HEDVIG. (*At the kitchen door.*) Mother, hadn't I better—? (*Sees HIALMAR, gives a loud scream of joy, and runs to him.*) Oh, father, father!

HIALMAR. (*Turns away and makes a gesture of repulsion.*). Away, away, away! (*To GINA.*) Keep her away from me, I say!

GINA. (*In a low tone.*) Go into the sitting-room, Hedvig.

HEDVIG *does so without a word.*

HIALMAR. (*Fussily pulls out the table-drawer.*) I must have my books with me. Where are my books?

GINA. Which books?

HIALMAR. My scientific books, of course; the technical magazines I require for my invention.

GINA. (*Searches in the bookcase.*) Is it these here paper-covered ones?

HIALMAR. Yes, of course.

GINA. (*Lays a heap of magazines on the table.*) Shan't I get Hedvig to cut them for you?

HIALMAR. I don't require to have them cut for me.

Short silence.

GINA. Then you're still set on leaving us, Ekdal?

HIALMAR. (*Rummaging amongst the books.*) Yes, that is a matter of course, I should think.

GINA. Well, well.

HIALMAR. (*Vehemently.*) How can I live here, to be stabbed to the heart every hour of the day?

GINA. God forgive you for thinking such vile things of me.

HIALMAR. Prove—!

GINA. I think it's you as has got to prove.

HIALMAR. After a past like yours? There are certain claims—I may almost call them claims of the ideal—

GINA. But what about grandfather? What's to become of him, poor dear?

HIALMAR. I know my duty; my helpless father will come with me. I am going out into the town to make arrangements—H'm—(*hesitatingly.*)—has any one found my hat on the stairs?

GINA. No. Have you lost your hat?

HIALMAR. Of course I had it on when I came in last night; there's no doubt about that; but I couldn't find it this morning.

GINA. Lord help us! where have you been to with those two ne'er-do-weels?

HIALMAR. Oh, don't bother me about trifles. Do you suppose I am in the mood to remember details?

GINA. If only you haven't caught cold, Ekdal——

Goes out into the kitchen.

HIALMAR. (*Talks to himself in a low tone of irritation, whilst he empties the table-drawer.*) You're a scoundrel, Relling!—You're a low fellow!—Ah, you shameless tempter!—I wish I could get some one to stick a knife into you!

He lays some old letters on one side, finds the torn document of yesterday, takes it up and looks at the pieces; puts it down hurriedly as GINA *enters.*

GINA. (*Sets a tray with coffee, etc., on the table.*) Here's a drop of something hot, if you'd fancy it. And there's some bread and butter and a snack of salt meat.

HIALMAR. (*Glancing at the tray.*) Salt meat? Never under this roof! It's true I have not had a mouthful of solid food for nearly twenty-four hours; but no matter.—My memoranda! The commencement of my autobiography! What has become of my diary, and all my important papers? (*Opens the sitting-room door but draws back.*) She is there too!

GINA. Good Lord! the child must be somewhere!

HIALMAR. Come out.

He makes room, HEDVIG *comes, scared, into the studio.*

HIALMAR. (*With his hand upon the door-handle, says to* GINA.): In these, the last moments I spend in my former home, I wish to be spared from interlopers——

Goes into the room.

HEDVIG. (*With a bound towards her mother, asks softly, trembling.*) Does that mean me?

GINA. Stay out in the kitchen, Hedvig; or, no—you'd best go into your own room. (*Speaks to* HIALMAR *as she goes in to him.*) Wait a bit, Ekdal; don't rummage so in the drawers; I know where everything is.

HEDVIG. (*Stands a moment immovable, in terror and perplexity, biting her lips to keep back the tears; then she clenches her hands convulsively, and says softly.*): The wild duck.

She steals over and takes the pistol from the shelf, opens the garret door a little way, creeps in, and draws the door to after her. HIALMAR *and* GINA *can be heard disputing in the sitting-room.*

HIALMAR. (*Comes in with some manuscript books and old loose papers, which he lays upon the table.*) That portmanteau is of no use! There are a thousand and one things I must drag with me.

GINA. (*Following with the portmanteau.*) Why not leave all the rest for the present, and only take a shirt and a pair of woollen drawers with you?

HIALMAR. Whew!—all these exhausting preparations—!

Pulls off his overcoat and throws it upon the sofa.

GINA. And there's the coffee getting cold.

HIALMAR. H'm.

Drinks a mouthful without thinking of it, and then another.

GINA. (*Dusting the backs of the chairs.*) A nice job you'll have to find such another big garret for the rabbits.

HIALMAR. What! Am I to drag all those rabbits with me too?

GINA. You don't suppose grandfather can get on without his rabbits.

HIALMAR. He must just get used to doing without them. Have not I to sacrifice very much greater things than rabbits!

GINA. (*Dusting the bookcase.*) Shall I put the flute in the portmanteau for you?

HIALMAR. No. No flute for me. But give me the pistol!

GINA. Do you want to take the pigstol with you?

HIALMAR. Yes. My loaded pistol.

GINA. (*Searching for it.*) It's gone. He must have taken it in with him.

HIALMAR. Is he in the garret?

GINA. Yes, of course he's in the garret.

HIALMAR. H'm—poor lonely old man.

He takes a piece of bread and butter, eats it, and finishes his cup of coffee.

GINA. If we hadn't have let that room, you could have moved in there.

HIALMAR. And continued to live under the same roof with—! Never,—never!

GINA. But couldn't you put up with the sitting-room for a day or two? You could have it all to yourself.

HIALMAR. Never within these walls!

GINA. Well then, down with Relling and Molvik.

HIALMAR. Don't mention those wretches' names to me! The very thought of them almost takes away my appetite.—Oh no, I must go out into the storm and the snow-drift,—go from house to house and seek shelter for my father and myself.

GINA. But you've got no hat, Ekdal! You've been and lost your hat, you know.

HIALMAR. Oh those two brutes, those slaves of all the vices! A hat must be procured. (*Takes another piece of bread and butter.*) Some arrangements must be made. For I have no mind to throw away my life, either.

Looks for something on the tray.

GINA. What are you looking for?

HIALMAR. Butter.

GINA. I'll get some at once.

Goes out into the kitchen.

HIALMAR. (*Calls after her.*) Oh it doesn't matter; dry bread is good enough for me.

GINA. (*Brings a dish of butter.*) Look here; this is fresh churned.

She pours out another cup of coffee for him; he seats himself on the sofa, spreads more butter on the already buttered bread, and eats and drinks awhile in silence.

HIALMAR. Could I, without being subject to intrusion—intrusion of any sort—could I live in the sitting-room there for a day or two?

GINA. Yes, to be sure you could, if you only would.

HIALMAR. For I see no possibility of getting all father's things out in such a hurry.

GINA. And, besides, you've surely got to tell him first as you don't mean to live with us others no more.

HIALMAR. (*Pushes away his coffee cup.*) Yes, there is that too; I shall have to lay bare the whole tangled story to him—I must turn matters over; I must have breathing-time; I cannot take all these burdens on my shoulders in a single day.

GINA. No, especially in such horrible weather as it is outside.

HIALMAR. (*Touching* WERLE'S *letter*.) I see that paper is still lying about here.

GINA. Yes, I haven't touched it.

HIALMAR. So far as I am concerned it is mere waste paper—

GINA. Well, I have certainly no notion of making any use of it.

HIALMAR.—but we had better not let it get lost all the same;—in all the upset when I move, it might easily—

GINA. I'll take good care of it, Ekdal.

HIALMAR. The donation is in the first instance made to father, and it rests with him to accept or decline it.

GINA. (*Sighs*.) Yes, poor old father—

HIALMAR. To make quite safe—Where shall I find some gum?

GINA. (*Goes to the bookcase*.) Here's the gum-pot.

HIALMAR. And a brush?

GINA. The brush is here too.

Brings him the things.

HIALMAR. (*Takes a pair of scissors*.) Just a strip of paper at the back—(*Clips and gums*.) Far be it from me to lay hands upon what it not my own—and least of all upon what belongs to a destitute old man—and to—the other as well.—There now. Let it lie there for a time; and when it is dry, take it away. I wish never to see that document again. Never!

GREGERS WERLE *enters from the passage.*

GREGERS. (*Somewhat surprised*.) What,—are you sitting here, Hialmar?

HIALMAR. (*Rises hurriedly*.) I had sunk down from fatigue.

GREGERS. You have been having breakfast, I see.

HIALMAR. The body sometimes makes its claims felt too.

GREGERS. What have you decided to do?

HIALMAR. For a man like me, there is only one course possible. I am just putting my most important things together. But it takes time, you know.

GINA. (*With a touch of impatience.*) Am I to get the room ready for you, or am I to pack your portmanteau?

HIALMAR. (*After a glance of annoyance at* GREGERS.) Pack—and get the room ready!

GINA. (*Takes the portmanteau.*) Very well; then I'll put in the shirt and the other things.

Goes into the sitting-room and draws the door to after her.

GREGERS. (*After a short silence.*) I never dreamed that this would be the end of it. Do you really feel it a necessity to leave house and home?

HIALMAR. (*Wanders about restlessly.*) What would you have me do?—I am not fitted to bear unhappiness, Gregers. I must feel secure and at peace in my surroundings.

GREGERS. But can you not feel that here? Just try it. I should have thought you had firm ground to build upon now—if only you start afresh. And, remember, you have your invention to live for.

HIALMAR. Oh don't talk about my invention. It's perhaps still in the dim distance.

GREGERS. Indeed!

HIALMAR. Why, great heavens, what would you have me invent? Other people have invented almost everything already. It becomes more and more difficult every day—

GREGERS. And you have devoted so much labour to it.

HIALMAR. It was that blackguard Relling that urged me to it.

GREGERS. Relling?

HIALMAR. Yes, it was he that first made me realise my aptitude for making some notable discovery in photography.

GREGERS. Aha—it was Relling!

HIALMAR. Oh, I have been so truly happy over it! Not so much for the sake of the invention itself, as because Hedvig believed in it—believed in it with a child's whole eagerness of faith.—At least, I have been fool enough to go and imagine that she believed in it.

GREGERS. Can you really think Hedvig has been false towards you?

HIALMAR. I can think anything now. It is Hedvig that stands in my way. She will blot out the sunlight from my whole life.

GREGERS. Hedvig! Is it Hedvig you are talking of? How should she blot out your sunlight?

HIALMAR. (*Without answering.*) How unutterably I have loved that child! How unutterably happy I have felt every time I came home to my humble room, and she flew to meet me, with her sweet little blinking eyes. Oh, confiding fool that I have been! I loved her unutterably;—and I yielded myself up to the dream, the delusion, that she loved me unutterably in return.

GREGERS. Do you call that a delusion?

HIALMAR. How should I know? I can get nothing out of Gina; and besides, she is totally blind to the ideal side of these complications. But to you I feel impelled to open my mind, Gregers. I cannot shake off this frightful doubt—perhaps Hedvig has never really and honestly loved me.

GREGERS. What would you say if she were to give you a proof of her love? (*Listens.*) What's that? I thought I heard the wild duck—?

HIALMAR. It's the wild duck quacking. Father's in the garret.

GREGERS. Is he? (*His face lights up with joy.*) I say you may yet have proof that your poor misunderstood Hedvig loves you!

HIALMAR. Oh, what proof can she give me? I dare not believe in any assurance from that quarter.

GREGERS. Hedvig does not know what deceit means.

HIALMAR. Oh Gregers, that is just what I cannot be sure of. Who knows what Gina and that Mrs. Sörby may many a time have sat here whispering and tattling about? And Hedvig usually has her ears open, I can tell you. Perhaps the deed of gift was not such a surprise to her, after all. In fact, I'm not sure but that I noticed something of the sort.

GREGERS. What spirit is this that has taken possession of you?

HIALMAR. I have had my eyes opened. Just you notice;—you'll see, the deed of gift is only a beginning. Mrs. Sörby has always been a good deal taken up with Hedvig; and now she has the power to do whatever she likes for the child. They can take her from me whenever they please.

GREGERS. Hedvig will never, never leave you.

HIALMAR. Don't be so sure of that. If only they beckon to her and throw out a golden bait—! And oh! I have loved her so unspeakably! I would have counted it my highest happiness to take her tenderly by the hand and lead her, as one leads a timid child through a great dark empty room!—I am cruelly certain now that the poor photographer in his humble attic has never really and truly been anything to her. She has only cunningly contrived to keep on a good footing with him until the time came.

GREGERS. You don't believe that yourself, Hialmar.

HIALMAR. That is just the terrible part of it—I don't know what to believe,—I never can know it. But can you really doubt that it must be as I say? Ho-ho, you have far too much faith in the claim of the ideal, my good Gregers! If those others came, with the glamour of wealth about them, and called to the child:—"Leave him: come to us: here life awaits you—!"

GREGERS. (*Quickly.*) Well, what then?

HIALMAR. If I then asked her: Hedvig, are you willing to renounce that life for me? (*Laughs scornfully.*) No thank you! You would soon hear what answer I should get.

A pistol shot is heard from within the garret.

GREGERS. (*Loudly and joyfully.*) Hialmar!

HIALMAR. There now; he must needs go shooting too.

GINA. (*Comes in.*) Oh Ekdal, I can hear grandfather blazing away in the garret by himself.

HIALMAR. I'll look in—

GREGERS. (*Eagerly, with emotion.*) Wait a moment! Do you know what that was?

HIALMAR. Yes, of course I know.

GREGERS. No you don't know. But I do. That was the proof!

HIALMAR. What proof?

GREGERS. It was a child's free-will offering. She has got your father to shoot the wild duck.

HIALMAR. To shoot the wild duck!

GINA. Oh, think of that—!

HIALMAR. What was that for?

GREGERS. She wanted to sacrifice to you her most cherished possession; for then she thought you would surely come to love her again.

HIALMAR. (*Tenderly, with emotion.*) Oh, poor child!

GINA. What things she does think of!

GREGERS. She only wanted your love again, Hialmar. She could not live without it.

GINA. (*Struggling with her tears.*) There, you can see for yourself, Ekdal.

HIALMAR. Gina, where is she?

GINA. (*Sniffs.*) Poor dear, she's sitting out in the kitchen, I dare say.

HIALMAR. (*Goes over, tears open the kitchen door, and says.*): Hedvig, come, come in to me! (*Looks around.*) No, she's not here.

GINA. Then she must be in her own little room.

HIALMAR. (*Without.*) No, she's not here either. (*Comes in.*) She must have gone out.

GINA. Yes, you wouldn't have her anywheres in the house.

HIALMAR. Oh, if she would only come home quickly, so that I can tell her—Everything will come right now, Gregers; now I believe we can begin life afresh.

GREGERS. (*Quietly.*) I knew it; I knew the child would make amends.

> OLD EKDAL *appears at the door of his room; he is in full uniform, and is busy buckling on his sword.*

HIALMAR. (*Astonished.*) Father! Are you there?

GINA. Have you been firing in your room?

EKDAL. (*Resentfully, approaching.*) So you go shooting alone, do you, Hialmar?

HIALMAR. (*Excited and confused.*) Then it wasn't you that fired that shot in the garret?

EKDAL. Me that fired? H'm.

GREGERS. (*Calls out to* HIALMAR.) She has shot the wild duck herself!

HIALMAR. What can it mean? (*Hastens to the garret door, tears it aside, looks in and calls loudly.*): Hedvig!

GINA. (*Runs to the door.*) Good God, what's that!

HIALMAR. (*Goes in.*) She's lying on the floor!

GREGERS. Hedvig! lying on the floor!

    Goes in to HIALMAR

GINA. (*At the same time.*) Hedvig! Inside the garret, No, no, no!

EKDAL. Ho-ho! does she go shooting, too, now?

    HIALMAR, GINA *and* GREGERS *carry* HEDVIG *into the studio; in her dangling right hand she holds the pistol fast clasped in her fingers.*

HIALMAR. (*Distracted.*) The pistol has gone off. She has wounded herself. Call for help! Help!

GINA. (*Runs into the passage and calls down.*) Relling! Relling! Doctor Relling; come up as quick as you can!

    HIALMAR *and* GREGERS *lay* HEDVIG *down on the sofa.*

EKDAL. (*Quietly.*) The woods avenge themselves.

HIALMAR. (*On his knees beside* HEDVIG.) She'll soon come to now. She's coming to— ; yes, yes, yes.

GINA. (*Who has come in again.*) Where has she hurt herself? I can't see anything—

    RELLING *comes hurriedly, and immediately after him* MOLVIK; *the latter without his waistcoat and necktie, and with his coat open.*

RELLING. What's the matter here?

GINA. They say Hedvig has shot herself.

HIALMAR. Come and help us!

RELLING. Shot herself!

    He pushes the table aside and begins to examine her.)

HIALMAR. (*Kneeling and looking anxiously up at him.*) It can't be dangerous? Speak, Relling! She is scarcely bleeding at all. It can't be dangerous?

RELLING. How did it happen?

HIALMAR. Oh, we don't know—

GINA. She wanted to shoot the wild duck.

RELLING. The wild duck?

HIALMAR. The pistol must have gone off.

RELLING. H'm. Indeed.

EKDAL. The woods avenge themselves. But I'm not afraid, all the same.

Goes into the garret and closes the door after him.

HIALMAR. Well, Relling,—why don't you say something?

RELLING. The ball has entered the breast.

HIALMAR. Yes, but she's coming to!

RELLING. Surely you can see that Hedvig is dead.

GINA. (*Bursts into tears.*) Oh my child, my child—

GREGERS. (*Huskily.*) In the depths of the sea—

HIALMAR. (*Jumps up.*) No, no, she must live! Oh, for God's sake, Relling—only a moment—only just till I can tell her how unspeakably I loved her all the time!

RELLING. The bullet has gone through her heart. Internal hemorrhage. Death must have been instantaneous.

HIALMAR. And I! I hunted her from me like an animal! And she crept terrified into the garret and died for love of me! (*Sobbing.*) I can never atone to her! I can never tell her—! (*Clenches his hands and cries, upwards.*) O thou above—! If thou be indeed! Why hast thou done this thing to me?

GINA. Hush, hush, you mustn't go on that awful way. We had no right to keep her, I suppose.

MOLVIK. The child is not dead, but sleepeth.

RELLING. Bosh.

HIALMAR. (*Becomes calm, goes over to the sofa, folds his arms, and looks at HEDVIG.*) There she lies so stiff and still.

RELLING. (*Tries to loosen the pistol.*) She's holding it so tight, so tight.

GINA. No, no, Relling, don't break her fingers; let the pigstol be.

HIALMAR. She shall take it with her.

GINA. Yes, let her. But the child mustn't lie here for a show. She shall go to her own room, so she shall. Help me, Ekdal.

HIALMAR *and* GINA *take* HEDVIG *between them.*

HIALMAR. (*As they are carrying her.*) Oh, Gina, Gina, can you survive this!

GINA. We must help each other to bear it. For now at least she belongs to both of us.

MOLVIK. (*Stretches out his arms and mumbles.*) Blessed be the Lord; to earth thou shalt return; to earth thou shalt return—

RELLING. (*Whispers.*) Hold your tongue, you fool; you're drunk.

HIALMAR *and* GINA *carry the body out through the kitchen door.* RELLING *shuts it after them.* MOLVIK *slinks out into the passage.*

RELLING. (*Goes over to* GREGERS *and says.*): No one shall ever convince me that the pistol went off by accident.

GREGERS. (*Who has stood terrified, with convulsive twitchings.*) Who can say how the dreadful thing happened?

RELLING. The powder has burnt the body of her dress. She must have pressed the pistol right against her breast and fired.

GREGERS. Hedvig has not died in vain. Did you not see how sorrow set free what is noble in him?

RELLING. Most people are ennobled by the actual presence of death. But how long do you suppose this nobility will last in him?

GREGERS. Why should it not endure and increase throughout his life?

RELLING. Before a year is over, little Hedvig will be nothing to him but a pretty theme for declamation.

GREGERS. How dare you say that of Hialmar Ekdal?

RELLING. We will talk of this again, when the grass has first withered on her grave. Then you'll hear him spouting about "the child too early torn from her father's heart;" then you'll see him steep himself in a syrup of sentiment and self-admiration and self-pity. Just you wait!

112

GREGERS. If you are right and I am wrong, then life is not worth living.

RELLING. Oh, life would be quite tolerable, after all, if only we could be rid of the confounded duns that keep on pestering us, in our poverty, with the claim of the ideal.

GREGERS. (*Looking straight before him.*) In that case, I am glad that my destiny is what is.

RELLING. May I inquire,—what is your destiny?

GREGERS. (*Going.*) To be the thirteenth at table.

RELLING. The devil it is.

THE END

LaVergne, TN USA
11 August 2010
192953LV00004B/81/P

9 781420 930856